EMILIO AMBASZ
THE POETICS OF THE PRAGMATIC

ARCHITECTURE, EXHIBIT, INDUSTRIAL AND GRAPHIC DESIGN

EMILIO AMBASZ
THE POETICS OF THE PRAGMATIC

ARCHITECTURE, EXHIBIT, INDUSTRIAL AND GRAPHIC DESIGN

ESSAYS BY

MARIO BELLINI
ALESSANDRO MENDINI
MICHAEL SORKIN
ETTORE SOTTSASS

RIZZOLI
NEW YORK

First published in the United States of America in 1988 by
Rizzoli International Publications, Inc.,
597 Fifth Avenue, New York, NY 10017

Library of Congress Cataloging-in-Publication Data

Ambasz, Emilio
  Emilio Ambasz: The Poetics of the Pragmatic
    p. cm.

  1. Ambasz, Emilio—Catalogs.   2. Architectural practice
International—New York (N.Y.)—Catalogs.
II. Title: Poetics of the Pragmatic.
NA839.A66Ad 1988   720'.92'4—dc19   88–42692 C
ISBN 0-8478-0966-8
ISBN 0-8478-0967-6 (pbk.)

Design: Bradford P. Collins, Group C, New Haven, Ct.

Set in type by Rainsford Type, Danbury, Ct.
Printed and bound in Japan by Dai Nippon Printing

Cover Illustration: Lucille Halsell Conservatory,
                San Antonio, Texas

CONTENTS

Essays

Ettore Sottsass

Mario Bellini

Alessandro Mendini

Michael Sorkin

Ettore Sottsass
Milan, Italy

When Emilio Ambasz came to Milan quite a few years ago, perhaps eighteen years ago, to organize for the Museum of Modern Art in New York what later became the landmark exhibition "Italy: The New Domestic Landscape," he called me and we met. He spoke quickly in an Italian complicated by a heavy accent. I could barely understand him; not because his Italian was not more than correct, or his thoughts less than lucid, but because of the lightning speed with which he presented his ideas. It seemed to me as if he never wanted to give time for sandy words to age into solid rocks; it seemed as if he never wanted to let a sentence consolidate and descend upon the table; it seemed as if he rather wanted to keep his intellectual visions suspended in mid-air, levitating high above the ground so that they would resemble wind, light, or faraway rumors more than a statement.

Even the cover of the catalog Emilio designed for that important exhibition reflected the same attitude.

He had the photographs of some objects of Italian design die-cut in outline, as separate shapes, running around loosely, here and there, between two folded sheets of vellum paper used as a dust jacket. These six or seven loose die-cut shapes, representing different products of Italian design, could assume different combinations: they could either move around freely, or they could stand apart, or allow themselves to become entangled, and it could happen that someone studying the cover might not understand anything, or that he might understand everything but just for a fleeting instant, or that, in some very special cases, he might gain an everlasting insight. But always, there was a feeling of constant instability, a feeling that, from one moment to another, the die-cut pieces would start moving apart, that everything would get out of focus, that nothing would allow itself to be pinned down, or, even less, to be touched, or, least of all, to be grasped.

I believe that such a quest for a constant state of fluidity, such a perception of existence as an ever changing process pervades everything that Emilio has ever designed.

In his architectural work, for example, there are almost never objects plainly resting on earth, as is usually the case in more conventional architecture where buildings are just a statement, and that is all. Emilio's architectural creations are a bit outside the earth and a bit inside it. They are like stone slabs emerging from the earth, or fissures cracking the earth open, rather than attempts at controlling the universe by means of logic or agreed upon signs. His is an architecture seeking, almost always, to represent the internal and eternal movement of an all encompassing planetary geology while at the same time respectfully reflecting local pulses, explosions, contractions, tempests, and deeply welled mysteries.

It is known that the planet is in a constant state of flux, that mountains are worn away, that valleys rise and also become lower, that geological strata slide, that sand drips into the sea, that vapors emerge from cracks in the earth, that waters hollow out their own ways, that winds promenade across the sky, that clouds go from oceans to deserts, that the state of the planet is liquid and gaseous and the solid crust of the earth navigates as a slow boat; and, I could, naturally, be wrong, but it seems to me that the idea of this universal karma is ever present in Emilio's work.

Some times from his architecture come vapors, and, sometimes, we can imagine it as if it were wrapped or covered by clouds or mist that make it appear and disappear, like the countries of the world as seen from a satellite. There is no architectural project Emilio has designed that is without water nearby, without wells, without lakes or without rivers.

But then, strangely, or perhaps not so, around Emilio's architecture there are never trees or forests, not even parks, as if trees, parks, and even the forests would already taste too much of human presence, of culture, or as one could say, of mental organization. Emilio's architectural landscapes seem to be the remnants of a place an hour after the great cataclysm, or, perhaps, I should rather say, a thousand hours after the cataclysm; those thousand hours that will have given time to Nature to calm itself and to assume the density of silence. After a thousand hours, man, or perhaps, technological superman, will have arrived to create order, to restructure some form of physical and mental survival; after such time, after a thousand hours, he may start to build a stairway leading who knows where, and to construct, here and there, some more or less useful arcade, some far away monument, some isolated little temple, and a few greenhouses to protect those last trees, those that have not been burned by the fires of the lava.

All these strange visions come to my mind when looking at his building for the San Antonio Botanical Garden, his terraces and entry lobby for the residential zone near Lugano, his project for a Cooperative of Chicano Grape Growers, his project for the Center for Applied Computer Research, his house in Cordoba, as well as many other projects Emilio has created.

Looking at all the projects, I have come to think that Emilio's buildings cannot with certainty be called monuments, even less can we call them literary exercises. By that I mean to say they are not exercises in architectural composition; they are not even intellectual conceits or objects; still less can one catalog them as attempts at technological rhetoric. I would call Emilio's architecture propitiatory designs seeking to invoke the presence of architecture. Each element of his edifices is a bit like a talismanic instrument of a wager, of a hidden ritual to fascinate some immense natural divinity. Maybe they are aspects of a liturgy, performed to obtain forgiveness for the scars we inflict everyday on the planet, or, maybe they are part of a magic ritual performed to establish harmony with those strange celestial rotations which Indians and Greeks, a long time ago, had already intuited.

This is a unique way of imagining architecture, certainly a new way, a special way, or perhaps it is a very ancient way. Perhaps this new way belongs to those very ancient times when, in order to found a city, an animal, perhaps a bull, was let free and the city became established wherever the bull, after a while, stopped to drink. In the same vein, I once heard from an old Sardinian shepard, many years ago, that the foundation of cities depended on the earth, that the place where a city is to emerge is already marked on the earth, because the place for the city is where deer, bison, and boar come together because there is water, or because there is shade, or because there is refuge from the winds.

Maybe the difference between the ancient propitiatory processes performed to secure the planet's good will — and then that of the whole universe — and those new propitatory proceses Emilio performs today lies only in the different technologies and in the different gestures he uses to satisfy archetypal longings. Truly, rituals take their form from the available technologies. In both a glass of Indian *soma* that one might drink to undertake a journey in spaces beyond daily ones, and a ride in an interplanetary ship to reach, more or less, the same destination, there is a great and beautiful jump. Certainly Emilio does not invoke the *soma* to design his architecture, neither does he drink it, or follow the hermetic rules of some complicated theological formula, as followed, for example, in building the Milan Cathedral. While the ultimate goal may be the same, his materials are different. He utilizes statistical calculations, new sources of light, electronic and optical fibers, artificial gases, telephones, chemically created materials never seen before, bonding agents, mist machines, unexpected fluorescent colors, laser rays, seismographers, invisible wells, silver plated balls, ultra-fast cements, and impermeable cardboard.

I know very well that Emilio does not drink Indian *soma* but uses all that so-called technological baggage that the contemporary world has put at our disposal. Moreover, I also know that sometimes Emilio is, if I may say so without being misunderstood, a devout, but, I must add, critical believer in the Technological Idea. Like very few architects, he senses the emergence of a technological mythology, fully aware of all that it may bring with it. I also know that he is very knowledgeable and that with relentless precision and painstaking patience he pays attention, as do very few, to the possibilities of technology as an irreplaceable device for bringing about that rare existential event that is architecture.

All of this I know already, and all of this that I know is also known by others, as we also know that it is not here that the root of his great originality lies. The thing which is original with Emilio, and which is very rare, is that technology is for him an instrument for suggesting architectural presences; that for him it is the architectural event, when it occurs, which serves as the magical instrument to bring about that still larger and even more complex event which is our spiritual existence. I imagine Emilio Ambasz to be a man outside the norm, at the cutting edge, and therefore, under surveillance. I see him as an imaginative and illuminated young man, resembling some old Chinese priest who, first for months, and then for years, uses ancient techniques to polish the surface of a great disk of green jade which will allow him, perhaps, to penetrate beyond the daily, or better still, which will allow him, even for just an instant, to place daily existence in some exalted architectural domain.

Mario Bellini
Milan, Italy

Emilio Ambasz, born in Argentina, lives now in the USA, but works everywhere: Europe, Asia and in the Americas. He is an architect and designer of unique relevance on the international scene.

His very special relationship with Italy started in 1972, when he conceived, directed and installed for the Museum of Modern Art in New York, the landmark exhibition "Italy: The New Domestic Landscape," which, together with the famous catalogue of the same name, which he edited, has remained a historical reference point for the study and understanding of Italian design since the Second World War.

Today, like many of his Italian colleagues, Ambasz practices his many professions in a manner completely different from that of the traditional American architectural office, which is generally segmented into very specialized and circumscribed fields. His activities range from architecture to landscape design, from graphic to industrial design, from interior design to the creation of furniture, while encompassing among other activities, urban planning, criticism, and an expertise in industrial manufacturing processes. This is not meant to imply a dilettante's approach or a diluted concentration. On the contrary, one may say that in practically every one of his fields, Emilio has achieved extraordinary results, as evidenced by his many accomplishments and awards. Some time ago, I learned that he had even been awarded the Prize Jean de la Fontaine for his "Working Fables." It does not surprise me; the subtlety and intelligence of his criticism and written comments are well known.

I still remember the surprise that arose from his unexpected entry into the Italian design scene when, in June of 1976, we learned that, in addition to his already renowned image as Curator of Design at the Museum of Modern Art, he had also achieved the distinction of being the creator of the Vertebra chair, a chair he originated, and then designed and developed in collaboration with G. Piretti. Vertebra was the first automatic, articulated office chair in the world.

On this occasion, as with the many others which followed, the importance of his achievement was immediately evident to all. We were not being presented with yet another variation from the large catalog of ergonomic office chairs; Vertebra represented a new and important re-evaluation of the notion of ergonomic seating, to such an extent that it dated everything that had been done before. It was, and is, the reference point for everything that has been designed in its field since.

The great merit of Vertebra consists of leaving behind the notion of the user having to constantly utilize levers and buttons in order to change the configuration of his chair, thus making it possible for the user to consider the chair as a dynamic and active entity, changing it's configuration automatically, whenever the body desires.

Even today, after so many years, we still perceive the importance of the changes brought about by Vertebra. The chair has become the standard for any other further improvement in design. It has influenced even the all-important German school of ergonomic seating design, which has in the last years seen a shift form the user manipulated chairs, characteristic of the last years of German seating design, towards Ambasz's notion of automatic and flexible seating. (This latter change is due in no small part, to the collaboration of the German furniture industry with non-German designers.)

Vertebra has made it evident that the most important service an office chair can provide is that of allowing the dorsal spine to articulate in the lumbar area rather than in that of the femur, which has been, in the past, the way other chairs have tried to achieve a certain degree of movement. In short, the articulation Vertebra provides at the lumbar position is the ideal one, since it does not engage the abdominal muscles and allows the user to exercise the inter-vertebral discs, thereby actively maintaining the flowing of fluids in the dorsal spine.

In the same way that Ambasz's basic concept for Vertebra impressed us all, it seems to me that we will never get used to his omnipresent design ability. It is both stimulating, as well as slightly frightening, to know that at this very moment, in some part of the world, he is designing yet another project or inventing another concept that may, once again, bring about a momentous change in design.

Alesandro Mendini
Milan, Italy

I do not know who Emilo Ambasz is. As a man and as an artist, he answers to no predictable pattern. He is, first, a man who shields his tenderness with a transparent layer of aggressiveness plated over his substantial timidity. Second, he is an exquisite poet. Then he is a land artist, then a farmer-cum-engineer cast in a biblical mold, a boundless juggler, a pioneer who suggests the image of mythologies yet to come, and finally the designer of sophisticated terrestrial paradises for modern times. Or, perhaps, I am absolutely wrong, and he may be, instead, a skillful and insightful observer of macro-economics who also invents complex mechanisms while listening to Monteverdi's music. Or, he may be a playwright who spreads over our global memories of vanished worlds. Perhaps he is a prophet, obstinately setting himself in the role of

"Anti Master." Or, maybe he is an empirical genius, as seen, for example, when he endowed the office chair with Vertebra. Or maybe his projects, as large as unpolluted continents or as small as flexible ball point pens, play a game of running away from us and from themselves, resembling a bed of self-deprecating Narcissuses that project on the water their own alternately self-admiring and self-amused image.

The seduction by Emilio's projects comes about from relegating man-made culturally conditioned forms and colors to the background in order to favor meadows, lakes, valleys, flowers, sunsets, suspended gardens, and skies with colors like Tiepolo's white, blue, green and gold. Thus, not only as an artist but also as a person, Emilio is a "unique case." Impossible to pin down, impossible to classify, he continually appears in a different guise. An inexhaustible inventor of metaphors — blue prince of his own fables — he is also the mystical master of ceremonies of a ritual, of a liturgy, and of an astrology created by himself. Thus, Emilio grants us only one certainty: that of his absolute singularity and originality. Seemingly devoid of ancestors and an orphan of cultural echoes, he condenses dramas and contradictions behind his only visible traits: the ironic but tragic, the hard but fragile, the sarcastic but loving countenances of this cordial and naturally polite gentleman — something of a knight of the supersonic era. He seems to be the ancient and archaic child whom I imagine dressed in a three piece suit, forced to play the precocious, lonely adult. Today, he is an adult rich in experience, but he has kept a child's eyes full of wonder. In order to get to know him (an enterprise which, I insist, is an impossible achievement) one must start the voyage from his artistic intuition rather than try to deal with his excessive intelligence; we must look at the fabric of his existence rather than search for the sure certainty of his projects.

Emilio is a ubiquitous being: his *genius loci* is the entire planet. In the same day he can think about and live in New York, in Asia, in Europe and in Latin America. Thus, we cannot follow his life which automatically is both wrapped in legend and mystery; it is like that of a cat we see dreaming on top of the mantlepiece, playing outside the doorstep, and hiding under the bed seemingly all at once. How is it possible, truly, to get to know a being of infinite mobility? Different spirits inhabit the body of Emilio. They come out in the morning, like birds from the nest, flying their separate ways toward far away universes to exercise their empirical magic, to resolve needs, to achieve enchanted experiences. They then return to be greeted, recharged, and find protection within their common nest, their "strong container" Mr. Ambasz.

This gentleman, this playwright actor, this cat, this child, this little bird, this nest — as a person, as a professional, and as an artist, is then, I must repeat, a unique case. His very large and complex body of work doesn't seem to seek the friendship of academy, nor care to contribute to the canonical history of architecture, design and language. It seems, rather, to be born from an obsessive search for primary principles, from a careful and wise observation of the surrounding reality, from an identification of humanistic problems perceived as only a hypersensitive instrument such as Emilio can — a sort of imaginative and scrupulous sensing device that gets to the core of all questions, that strives to satiate the essential quest for techniques and images that men have, that registers the original sense of beginning as well as the anthropological and ecological tremors of a modern world. The passion and pragmatism he offers in opposition to prevailing simple minded functionalism is, perhaps, a result of his direct lineage or ancestral connection to the Cyclopean anti-monumentalism of Buckminster Fuller. The work of Emilio is not post-Modern. His vocabulary is not made up of references and ready made sentences; thus it is free of the decay of fashions and styles. He proposes as principle and method, as archetypal idea, pure and primary, the notion that an arch is an arch, is an arch; that a man is a man, is a man; and that a house is a concept that should contain both its past and its future, the beginning and the end of all our dwelling memories, whether true or imagined.

More fascinated with seeds than with fully grown entities, Emilio's game is more suited to the practitioner of genetics than to the traditional architect. It consists of solving functions and satisfying requirements without having to build a corresponding object. It consists of making architecture, but without just erecting buildings — a sort of architecture that is and isn't. It consists of designing prototypical and conceptual structures instead of stylistic ones. It rests not in the search for the optimal and definitive design of an artifact, but in the utopia of constantly re-designing, seeking to resemble Nature itself. From such a quest stem the material elements which constitute the repertoire of his "non-style" windmills, transparent greenhouses, floating barges, vanishing clouds of mist on top of piazzas, climbing plants creating entrance gates, and the calligraphic signs (not dissimilar to Kandinski's little snakes or viruses under a microscope) that embroider terse meadows where invisible villas emerge from the ground like fulfilled submarines.

Perhaps after the efforts we have undertaken to understand him, a few strong messages begin to emerge from our magician's top hat. Emilio believes deeply that architecture and design are mythical acts. He proposes a different, emotional method, a passionate and sensual mode of existence. His thoughts and images are based on the primitive but eternal process of being born, falling in love and dying — those things that have always moved the world, those irreducible drives that always return. Who then is Emilio? He is a dreamer who dedicates heart and soul to men while longing for angels. Or perhaps . . .

Et In Arcadia Emilio
By Michael Sorkin

Fancy spreads Edens whereso'er they be;

The world breaks on them like an opening flower,

Green joys and cloudless skys are all they see;

The hour of childhood is a rose's hour. . . .

John Clare, *Joys of Childhood.*

"The Aleph?" I repeated.

"Yes, the only place on earth where all places are seen from every angle, each standing clear, without any confusion or blending."

Borges, *The Aleph.*

"My chief problem in writing the story lay in what Walt Whitman had very successfully achieved—the setting down of a limited catalogue of endless things."

Borges, commenting on *The Aleph.*

Emilio Ambasz also compiles catalogs of the ineffable. Patiently, he works to materialize a recurrent idyll of place, mapping and remapping his private order of signs, bringing into view his halcyon world. "Emilio's Folly" is a likely Aleph, a summary offered with the full certification of the unconscious. Ambasz offers a canny origin tale: "I never thought about it by means of words. It came to me as an image: full-fledged, clear and irreducible." Full-fledged, certainly, for housing the recurring repertoire of Ambasz's imagery, a lexical dream.

First, the landscape: pampas or prairie is the literal or conceptual setting for virtually all of Ambasz's architectural work, his mental elysium. Swarded green, pastures of plenty rolling to infinity, there's a parity among all that grows in this fertility. But metaphor translates imprecisely to morphology. If his inserted architectural particulars are not exactly biomorphic, they're nevertheless naturalized as growths, geological, ordered rifts and crystals thrusting up from some subterranean lode.

Then, the sky. Ambasz once confided to me that the key to successful architectural presentation lies in beautifully photographed models. He once explained that such representation could only be obtained from the photographer with "the best sky." I liked the idea that the priesthood of simulation held a wizard-proprietor of the sky, Acteon with a Nikon. As Ambasz's green plains merge along a faint horizon with that perfect blue heaven, a universe shimmers to life, like a photograph emerging from emulsion, an Aleph under its all-encompassing dome.

Not to belabor the metaphor, Ambasz's architecture is preoccupied with the procreative cycle. Habitation inevitably occupies a cave-like subterranean space. In the "Folly," these caves are the repositories of the totems of childhood: kids are "mnemosyne and heard." Fertility symbols abound. That lone lemon, flung up on its baldachin to signal the folly's entry, invites bent-kneed druids at sun-up. The mountain, pushing from the square terrestrial orifice, is unmistakable. And the architect, poling himself across the amniotic expanse, re-enters the primal scene, to peer up the mountain's shaft at clouds scudding over its "zenithal opening," and departs via "a man height tunnel leading to an open pit filled with a fresh mist."

"Heaven lies about us in our childhood," wrote Wordsworth. Ambasz's architecture privileges a retrieval of simplicity, a paring down, the integrity of innocence. His geometry is of abiding directness, favoring squares, triangles, circles, used with little complication. Fervently minimalist, his interventions in the landscape investigate the signification of the least, the smallest sign suitable to materialize architecture. At the house in Cordoba, two vertical planes intersect. At the Schlumberger project in Texas, the landscape is animated by squiggly lines and a spray of tiny tempictti. This is architecture aiming at a kind of divinity, a vision of paradise, Emilio in Wonderland. In this technicolor dream of the world, architecture merely annotates, inscribes godly doodles on a near perfect terrain, punctuated with tiny classicisms.

This vision is not distant from another origin-absorbed architect's. "May I take you to the shores of a mountain lake," he wrote. "The sky is blue, the water is green, and everything is at peace. The mountains and the clouds are reflected in the lake, as are the houses, farms and chapels. They stand there as if they had never been built by human hands. They look as if they have come from God's own workshop, just like the mountains and the trees, the clouds and the blue sky. And everything radiates beauty and quiet. . . . "

The writer, of course, was Adolf Loos, an earlier avatar of the architecture of the indigenous spirit. It was a sensibility he conceded to both the farmer (like Ambasz, the unmediated dreamer) who builds directly from the unconscious and the engineer whose constructions he held to be similarly naturalized. Loos—fixated with tomb and monument, longing for a return to origins, enamored of America, mesmerized by technology and nature both, and derogator of ornament—is one of Ambasz's unmistakeable ances-

tors. The passage of half a century permits the continuation of his ideas, but the sting's out now. Ambasz—

the gentle Argentinian—is a fabulist, not a polemicist, but there's a vision which persists, a common idea

seen from another side.

Ambasz aphorizes: "Europe's eternal quest remains Utopia, the myth of the end. America's returning

myth is Arcadia, the eternal beginning." Arcadia's is the social version of childhood, the innocent interlude

before the fall. While Arcadia is certainly the central myth in Ambasz's doxology of cultural renewal, it

isn't precisely the muzzy standard Arcadian dream. Formed, though he was, in the sixties, he's no hippie.

Ambasz continues, "the traditional vision of Arcadia is that of a humanistic garden. America's arcadia has

turned into a man made nature, a forest of artificial trees and mental shadows."

Here's the opening through which the machine is invited to enter the garden. An abiding American

type—intact from Jefferson to Horatio Greenough and down to silicon valley tinkers casting their mental

shadows on electronic workbenches out back in the garage—is the democratic mechanic. This heroic per-

son differs both from Loos' instinctual farmer and his engineer, collapsing aspects of both. Ambasz once ar-

rogated the then-fashionable conceit of the bricoleur to describe his work and self. It's close to the truth:

the tribal handyman, tinkerer, collector of odds and ends. But the notion stands, in its anthropological

origins, at a myth-maker's remove from the facts. This exultation of instinct is a strategy, of course. Am-

basz is an artist of great deliberation. He prefers, however, the rhetoric of accident and innocence. Like

Thoreau, Wordsworth, Rousseau, or Lewis Carroll, he knows very well that childhood has a politics. I'm re-

minded, however, of two adult photographs—photos of Ambasz wearing, as it were, different hats. In the

first, it's a Greek fisherman's cap, a briefly popular variation on the generic worker's headgear that projects

Ambasz as humble craftsman, not unlike Whitman's famous portrait for *Leaves of Grass*. The second

photo has him in a slouched felt hat. The conceit now is of the private eye, the mental investigator, the pre-

ferred metaphor of inquiry for a skeptical age. The union seems emblematic of his apparently alternating

modes. His talent is reconciliation; he is the polyglot poet, speaking two tongues of modernity.

Ambasz has had the usual young architect's frustration in getting his schemes built, although this

hasn't sapped their influence. He has, however, enjoyed nothing but success as an industrial designer. A se-

ries of projects—most notably the "Vertebra" office chair, which he created and then developed with G. Pi-

retti—has placed him in the first rank of that disciplined discourse of design that grew in Italy in the 1960s and 70s. His own production grows from what was undoubtedly a seminal experience for Ambasz the designer: his curatorship of the Design Department at the Museum of Modern Art during the early and mid 1970s. As is well known, his most important show was "Italy: The New Domestic Landscape," a massive celebration of Italian modern design. For Ambasz, the bricoleur, collection is research, acclimation to a sensibility. And, he emerged from the show with his compulsions intact, ready to join a phenomenon he had himself ordered and codified.

The beautiful Vertebra chair (which has become one of Hollywood's preferred signifiers of modernity and post, swiveling in dozens of establishing shots) has by now become Ambasz's own Modulor. Of course, it appears, for scale and as advertisement, in many a magazine spread of Ambasz's interior design work, those classic unpopulated photographs in which occupation is not permitted to gainsay elegance. The Vertebra is the Modulor's mental shadow. Le Corbusier exhausted Mr. Modulor with the Venice Hospital project when he turned the totem on its side, and put it to bed. But Modulor was never able to sit down, to place itself in an attitude of anything but exuberance or repose. It's not insignificant that Ambasz is perhaps best known to the world as the architect of a marvelous machine for sitting, at last a comfortable place for the Modulor to get to work. A chair of infinite accommodation, expanding and contracting not as a seat of the Golden Mean but to support everyone in his or her slightly different requirements.

Ambasz loves mechanisms both as the obvious outcome of the mechanic's arts, and as a sort of surrogate citizenry. As his offices are populated with Vertebra, a metonomy that renders the furniture at least partially human, so his larger landscapes share this animating impulse. In Mexico, New Orleans, and Seville, elements float on artificial ponds, nominal boats, rationalized via the faded ethic of flexibility, but really so many mechanical ducks, going through the changes of a continuous picturesque reordering. The Mercedes Benz showroom is perhaps an even more sublime naturalizing of the machine's happy habitat in the steel garden: cars grazing like sheep on a terrain of pure, glowing artifice. Ambasz has produced some version of the pastoral indeed, a nirvana for the 1990s.

There's another way in which Ambasz's investigation of architecture and landscape is continuous with his mechanical design. Both investigations are strongly minimalist in character. Unquestionably, Ambasz's formation is broadly influenced by the heroic earth movers and outdoor minimizers of his approximate generation—Michael Heizer, Donald Judd, Carl Andre, Richard Serra, from whom he has absorbed the twin impulses of boldness and simplicity in the creation of "site specific" works of art.

But this litany of spare gesturalists hardly accounts for the machine work. Of course, the ghost in every machine, functionalism, rears its antecedent head. Functionalism, however, as it's been received in architecture, has seldom been about the machine's real issues, but simply about its image. Ambasz's machines are better than this, they're about what the engineers like to call "elegance." Art-world minimalism has always been studied in its abiding ignorance of complexity. Indeed, the compulsive repetition and relentless paring down were hostile to both technology and its demon elaborations. To the engineer—the object of Loos' reverie, Emilio in the cap—functionalist minimalism is not about being simple, it's about being concise.

It's a quality Ambasz's industrial design is especially rich in, not simply mechanically but expressively as well. The Vertebra chair, for example, is distinguished from its innumerable kith by the way in which it efficiently identifies and solves one of the few abiding problematics of ergonomic chair design: the structural integration of seat, back, and arms. Vertebra uses the arms as the structural link between seat and back, eliminating the most generically irritating redunduncy in office chair design. The success of the product is not simply in solving the issues of sitting, but in a shrewd vision of just the relevant question of elegance.

Ambasz further tempers his minimalisms with that mild Argentine sense of surreality. Bricolage, of course, is the very manufactury of the surreal, with its random juxtaposing of found objects. But bricolage has always been more conceit than reality in his work. The real affinity is with a specific class of surrealistic landscape, especially as rendered by the classicists of the genre, Delvaux, Magritte, and Dali. Under that contemplating blue sky, or within the strictures of mystified architecture (everybody's favored physical representation of mind—those rooms, those nooks, those crannies), strange things live, inept machines lounge, long shadows grow over a generic mental landscape. Ambasz, too, makes such landscapes, both on his unceasing plain and in his rehabilitations. At the Banque Lambert, perspective is forced on a wooden model of the exterior of the housing building, glowing mysteriously at the end of the banking floor, poised, for all appearances, about to burst into flame.

Surrealism, of course, is vision, not substance. The Hudson River school painted railroad trains puffing through Sylvania with an altogether different view. They may have felt perplexity but they lacked surrealism's animating irony, our century's own favored mode of coping. Ambasz is also no ironist: there's no suspicion mingled with his love of the elements of his work. Indeed, as Aldo Rossi might be said to clarify De

Chirico, so Ambasz absorbs the surreal landscape, purging it of its dark clouds. Equally, he pares his minimalism of the masculine aggressiveness that was its own dirty dark side. The architecture that results has the sweetness of a man unembittered. Not a bad vision of the world, this innocent, nurturing posture.

Ambasz aims at an architecture without threat. About the work is an abiding sense of the ecological, nature's own system of decorum. The sort of reticence about grade that the work persistently displays is part of this, a deference to Mother nature. In refusing to accept the elevational datum of the everyday, Ambasz clearly suggests that his places are to be the sites of special rituals, a condition emphasized by his particular concern for the act of entry, invariably accentuating the processional. The attitude persists even in his city projects. In the Plaza Mayor in Salamanca, for example, the new square is depressed, leaving tree-tops at grade, beckoning visitors into the sheltering terrain.

Ambasz's agricultural fixation strikes clear affinities with rosy nineteenth century romanticism and with its architectural translation via William Morris. The Co-operative of Mexican American Grape Growers and the gardens at Ludenhausen are both invested with the ritual ethic of growth and renewal. For Ambasz, ritual is program, architecture's armature of meaning. Clearly, the culture for which he would design is one that has its festivals at solstices and equinoxes, on the day of planting and the afternoon of the harvest. Ah, wilderness!

Alfred Kazin said of Thoreau that he made "nature his beloved, the perfect Other." And Whitman agrees—with his usual self-serving expansiveness—that "the universe has only one complete lover and that is the poet." Ambasz's preoccupations with Americanness are, in a direct sense, a tactic for the capture of nature in a specifying embrace, a form of courtship. Like any lover, he manfully avoids giving offense. Ambasz is Thoreau without *Civil Disobedience*: his work is a meditation on cooperation. The world he describes is one in which the social contract is modelled on the family, a series of ordered enclaves of voluntarily cooperating, like-minded individuals for whom myths retain the power to inspire the rhythms of days. The order of things reflects the order of society. As with the Shakers, those functionalists of the spirit, elegance is the only excess.

It seems most appropriate that Ambasz's major building—the Lucille Halsell Conservatory in San Antonio—should be an enclosed botanical garden, a series of greenhouses. The great greenhouse is one of the most mesmerizing architectural achievements of the nineteenth century, the coincidence of technological advance and the arrival of the modern view of nature. Their designers were, like Ambasz, hypnotized by the possibilities of paradise. Paradise, however, had received a politics from the Enlightenment, it was now utopia. Nature, newly taxonomized, had become rational. The great tropical islands under glass constructed during the period were theaters of nature, polemics of possibility counterposed to the drear of urbanization and industry. Of course, these zoos for nature also had a dark side, hymns to regulation, the first great modern theme parks.

San Antonio is Ambasz's first realized ideogram for the world. These beautiful gardens contain virtually all the elements present in his earlier "Folly" and developed in projects over the years. Punctuated landscape, entry through the earth, collonaded courtyard, captive water, artificial mountains—here the glass shapes bursting out of the ground—attenuated processional, mists, symbolic trees, "hieratic secular temples sitting serenely in the landscape;" all are found in this palpable paradise. The garden is truly Emilio's Aleph, the biosphere of his "infinite greatness of place."

Borges has been called a "cosmogonist without a theology," and the description also fits Ambasz well. His continual grasping after benign totality is filled with the inspirational poignancy and valor of the poet. Looking freshly for sources, his is the struggle to make architecture innocent. What happier preoccupation for an architect than to domesticate science, to make gardens, to "dream perfect dreams for us." Let Wordsworth's *Tintern Abbey* sum up:

Therfore am I still

A lover of the meadows and the woods,

And mountains; and of all that we behold

From this green earth; of all the mighty world

Of eye and ear, both what they half create

And what perceive; well pleased to recognize

In nature and the language of the sense,

The anchor of my purest thoughts, the nurse,

The guide, the guardian of my heart, and soul

Of all my moral being.

Dream on, Emilio.

I Ask Myself

Emilio Ambasz

It has always been my deep belief that architecture and design are both myth-making acts. I hold that their real tasks begin once functional and behavioral needs have been satisfied. It is not hunger, but love and fear, and sometimes wonder, that make us create. The architect's or designer's milieu may change, but the task remains the same: to give poetic form to the pragmatic.

On the one hand, I am playing with elements that come from my period, such as technology. On the other, I am proposing a different mode of existence. This is a search for essential things — being born, being in love, and dying — certain things which always move the heart, eternal things which always return. They have to do with existence on an emotional, passionate, and sensual level. Perhaps I use very austere elements to express these things, and therefore the gesture itself is austere — but in this way it may also be far more durable. It is certainly a classical attempt. I am interested in the passionate and the emotional in an almost timeless manner; I am interested in presenting examples that are like master examples.

How do you apply this passion for the enduring, almost universal archetype to the changeable demands and myriad contingencies of modern life?

If one finds the quintessence of a problem, one will have better access to an irreducible solution. The thread supporting my design quest in every area — my products and my architecture — is a single preoccupation: finding the root of the problem, its essence.

For example, in the case of the Vertebra chair, which looks like such a highly mechanized artifact, I was deeply concerned with creating an anthropomorphic and anthropofunctional object that accompanies the movement of the body completely and unselfconsciously, just as a glove moves with the hand that wears it. The chair was conceived as an extension of the body, and that was the underlying principle for its design. The appearance I gave the chair originally would be different today, since prevailing stylistic interests have changed, but the essential concept behind the articulated chair remains valid.

If it seems difficult to reconcile the appearance of Vertebra with that of some of my architectural projects, remember that men sit on chairs while they dwell in buildings. One deals with man in very different dimensions, and the further away one goes from his body into the social domain, the more design and architecture will change in respone to additional sets of demands.

Would you be more specific about the process through which you conduct such investigations and translate your discoveries into concrete designs?

I like to think that I have trained myself in a discipline for concentrating on the principle of the problem, thereby getting rid of all extraneous elements. Only rarely will I sketch a number of studies; those I do in my mind. Therefore, I never see a product or a house as sets of drawings, but rather as a three-dimensional entity I can hold before my mind's eye and turn around or move into. Once the mental image is formed, then, and only then, do I draw it up in one of the notebooks that I carry with me constantly. I usually draw it exactly as it will be, in plan, section, and elevation. And, in most cases, the only thing necessary for further development is to enlarge those sketches to the proper scale. These drawings become the working basis for the design-development phase that always follows the preliminary stage of design. This enables me to work anywhere and at any time (I like to say that I have offices not only in the U.S.A. and in Italy, but in airports all over the world). It is, of course, a solitary process, though after a result comes to light, I take the greatest pleasure in working with a team of people who may modify, alter, and enrich the project.

As I often tell my friends, "Emilio Ambasz" has two seemingly paradoxical selves within him: "Emilio" is a solitary, cheerful man, anguished nevertheless because he hopes through his architecture to be welcomed by angels; "Ambasz" is a sociably sad man, anxious because he wants his products to be well received by men. I, on the other hand, am cheerfully sad and sociably solitary.

This emblematic self-portrait calls to mind the fables that are yet another of your expressive repertoire. How do these parables, such as your Design Tales for Skeptic Children, *articulate additional aspects of your life and work?*

It has been said that despite my Argentine birth, there is something very North American about my attitude, about my distrust of the ideological and my apparently guileless predilection for simple truths. In one sense, I hope that my Tales keep childlike. The guilelessness, however, is only apparent. I opted to be a fabulist rather than an ideologist because fables retain the ring of immutability long after ideologies have withered. The invention of fables is central to my working methods; it is not just a literary accessory. Sometimes the fable is a project and the descriptive literary part is purely technical, and sometimes the imagery becomes the illustration. In any case, the subtext of a fable is a ritual, and it is to the support of rituals that most of my work addresses itself.

I am interested in rituals and ceremonies for the twenty-four hours of the day. I am not interested in rituals and ceremonies for very long voyages, voyages that can take forty or fifty years. Those are utopian. And what a tragedy to discover that for the sake of such long-term dreams we have sacrificed our daily lives. No, I am interested in daily rituals: the ritual of sitting in a courtyard, slightly protected from your neighbor's view and the strong wind, gazing up at the stars; the ritual of the father sitting on his bed and seeing his children playing in another room, across the courtyard — an acknowledgment that there exists a certain distance between generations, but with the hope that they may come together in some common space; an acceptance of the fact that the family unit exists, made up of people of different ages, with different modes of perception and different ways of seeing reality.

Or imagine this picture: He has a private space, She has a private space. They meet and reconcile themselves in the living room. The ideal arrangement, perhaps, would be two houses: He lives in one, She lives in the other, and they have to knock on the door if they want each other. They never take each other for granted.

Dealing with these types of situations attracts me. The ritual is not in the house; I don't make it. And yet the house provides a backdrop. I am fascinated by stage architecture, in the sense of its being a stage for daily life — not one that overwhelms you, but one you can somehow consciously understand.

Your references to utopian dreams and to drama recall criticism that has sometimes been leveled against your own architecture: that your projects are essentially beautiful visions.

What I design is grounded in carefully studied practical design and building decisions, supported by exhaustively researched working drawings covering structural, mechanical, and electrical systems, furnishings, and finishes. In fact, some of these projects have been built or are in the process of being built. Several projects described as "impossibly beautiful" in model form have actually been constructed. The San Antonio Botanical Garden, in Texas, is one such example. We must conclude, therefore, that they have become very "possible." In any case, when an artifact is described as beautiful, how much more "possibleness" can it ever aspire to?

A great deal of my time goes into proving that what I draw can be built and an important aspect of my design method is the use of readily available artifacts and techniques. My Mexican project, for instance, is composed of ready-mades: I could give you the names of all the manufacturers. The solar-energy panels were made in Mexico, the billboard in Holland, the barges in Mexico, the houses in France.

I consider my architecture an alternative to prevailing architectural pursuits. With land so precious and with ongoing concerns for finding ways of gracefully relating and juxtaposing the artificial to the natural, there might be found in my projects the seeds for a return to the roots of a genuinely balanced architecture as a form of man-made nature.

This stated mission obviously brings us to your extensive use of buildings apparently sunken into the earth. How does this device — still exotic to many observers — illustrate your avowed pragmatism?

I consider a glass curtain-wall building a great conceit, but not a properly insulated berm house, which requires little heating and returns the roof to the agricultural domain for further planting. In this regard, I see myself as far more practical than "bottom-line"-oriented architects and developers. The concept of the above-ground earth-covered building is a simple one, a very plain device. Some people get anxious about living close to the earth because they confuse berming with burial. Although many of my projects use earth, very few of them are underground. (In the Schlumberger project all buildings are built above grade, and only afterwards are some of their sides and roofs covered with a mantle of earth for insulation and to integrate them into the landscape.) I can take a normal house, a Levitt house, or even two trailers perpendicular to each other and cover them partially with earth, leaving sides open for direct view and ventilation. For projects of this sort I employ people who build swimming pools. They excavate up to the level where the house's foundations are going to rest and then the house is constructed in ordinary fashion. Waterproofing is the last step before extra earth is brought in and mounded against the walls.

You touched on the, to your mind, misguided association of such buildings with burial. What do you perceive to be the positive mythic or ritualistic dimension of this earth-sheltered architecture?

You always have the sense that behind the walls of these projects are absent presences or present absences. The notion of that which is in front of you and what happens behind the wall has always appealed to me. There is a certain anima or spirit behind the wall. The berms act as symbolic fortresses through which you pass to discover a terribly benign giant; yet they are simply hiding a very simple house. At the same time, I assume there are certain atavistic memories one senses while walking through masses of earth. You have an almost haptic perception of their density; you almost feel your hair is being pulled slightly. But the passageway is not an overwhelming tunnel, and the mass itself is designed in such a way that you know you will get through. I have no wish to provoke anguish. The feeling should be far more religious and, yes, ritualistic.

Do you in effect, then, invest architecture with a fetishistic power?

In my first such project, a house in Cordoba, I actually wanted to eliminate architecture. The only thing that was to stand was the facade, which would be like a mask, a surrogate for architecture. The architecture would disappear; you would see only the earth. You might say that by this device I seek, rhetorically, to eliminate architecture as a culturally conditioned process and return to the primeval notion of dwelling. I seek to develop an architectural vocabulary outside the canonical tradition of architecture. It is an architecture that is both here and not here. With it I hope to place the user in a new state of existence, a celebration of human majesty, thought, and sensation.

The ideal gesture would be to arrive at a plot of land which is so immensely fertile and welcoming that slowly the land would take shape to provide you with an abode. And within the abode, being such a magic space, it would never rain, nor would there ever be inclemencies of any other sort. We must build a house only because we are not welcome on the land. Every act of construction is a defiance of nature. In a perfect nature we wouldn't need houses. It's a hope, a millenarian hope.

Let's come back, though, to the here-and-now, to the "sociable" Ambasz you sketched earlier — the inventor eager to have his efforts welcomed by his contemporaries. How would he characterize the moment in history when he must build what he envisions? What are the myths we embody in the icons of our own era?

Since the beginning of the century there has been a concern with creating a new type of architecture. The ideological premise was that a new man would be the one stepping out of history, a new man emerging out of traditional class relationships. There would be a new system of property, of classes, and therefore there would be a new type of architecture. For fifty years, modern architecture tried not to relate to history at all. Then we realized that it was all a conceit of the mind, that we had lost a tremendous treasure of architectural experience. There was a longing for ornament, for sensual surfaces, for emotional experiences in architecture.

Professional architects have responded by turning to books of architecture for references. The so-called post-Modernists are, in most cases, very academic people, with a craving for footnoted quotations and a flawless scholastic method. They are frightened of inventing ornament because they are frightened of making images.

Ours is the only period in history that, instead of creating appropriate images to represent its myths, has developed methods for generating infinite images. So the image that best represents our period may be that of the method whereby such images may be generated — something like Sol LeWitt's formula for creating images without making a statement about a definite image. And thus you have architecture being taught as a method for generating architectural images without ever making a value judgment. No wonder it's hard for people in our culture to create conclusive, irreducible images; it would mean making value statements.

I have always believed that there are two types of histories. There is *kunstgeschichte* and there is *belles lettres*. I only believe in poetic criticism, mainly of the type that Baudelaire wrote, or of the sort that a great poet may write when commenting on another one; I have in mind Joseph Brodsky and his commentaries on the Russian poet Marina Tsvetaeva. As for my own feelings toward other living architects, I am happy to confess that I take an immense delight in their work. The more personal their song, the more I am fascinated by the bird. I would never design like Jim Stirling, but his work moves me; it is part of the substance from which I nourish myself. I take no interest in creating schools or fighting against other systems of thought. I only care for pleasure wherever it is architecturally possible and regardless of whomever made it.

Much of my work emphasizes classical concerns of architecture, such as the presence of light, the sound of water, manipulation of perspective, and the humane use of space to engender feelings of reassurance and hope. I am not against striving to maintain a continuum with history, nor am I against a search for ornament. I believe in inventing ornament when it comes from using natural materials, when it is intrinsic to the structure of the thing being made. I value this as a continuing process of discovery, not recovery. Architects returning to historical sources only to utilize elements that make sense to each other end up talking a hermetic language that can be understood only by those initiated into the cult. You can remain in this mode if you are content to stay within the convent, but you cannot solve real problems, such as housing, by cutting out little doorways and moldings and pasting them up to express a longing for modulated surfaces.

Sometimes, I confess, I fancy myself to be the last man of the present culture, building a house for the first man of a culture that has not yet arrived.

A Selection from

Working Fables
A Collection of Design Tales for Skeptic Children

By Emilio Ambasz

Fabula Rasa
1976

The little village was in the grip of fear; fear of Divine rages and of human passions. One of the men started to build a construction, circular in plan, cylindrical in volume, and with a domelike roof. He used stones, wood, and mud. His travails finished, he came back to tell the group the building he had erected was in the shape of the Universe and inside dwelt the Universe's Gods.

Then, using a rod he had taken from the temple, he made a circle around the village and with the help of others he encircled it with a high wall built of earth and stones. In the center of the village, next to the temple, he erected a large hut which he then covered completely, except for the entrance, with a mound of earth. On top of this mound he vertically placed six large stone slabs. That, he called his home. The others called it the palace.

When he died, his body was laid down inside the hut he had called his house, together with all his belongings, and his son covered the entrance with the large stone slabs he removed from the mound's top. Some people say this was how architecture started.

The Foundation of the House
1975

He went, and brought back a stone from his parent's house, drew the picture of a brick on a piece of paper, and carefully wrapped the stone in it. At sunrise, holding them high above his head, he walked along the diagonal lines of his land, and at their crossing, buried them both, still embraced. Facing the wind he spat as strongly as he could; turning around, he prayed for rain. With the mud he made walls at one end of his land. At the other end he wove a tightly knit wicker roof, and hung it from the trees. Having done all this, he walked away.

His children came back much later to take away stones for their own places. But, to some of these places, their own children never returned.

Anthology for a Spatial Buenos Aires
1966

The Mythological Foundation of Buenos Aires

It seems to me a tale that Buenos Aires ever started:

I judge her as eternal as the water and the sky.

Borges, *Cuaderno San Martin*

Limits

Buenos Aires has as limits the Rio de la Plata to the East, the Brook to the South, the Pampa to the West, and the Viceroyalty to the North. Two sides of water, one of past, one of future.

Sides? She has only four, for there are only four cardinal points. Four faces and two doors. Through the door of earth the country enters, through that of water, he goes out.

Martinez Estrada, *Las Cuatro Caras*

Sky

The Argentine sky? Yes, the sole great consolation. For I have seen this sky from the limitless Pampa, punctuated here and there by a few weeping willows, unlimited, shimmering in the day as in the night with a blue transparent light or swarming with stars. This celestial countryside is on the four horizons.

Le Corbusier, *Précisions*

Pampa

Pampa, Indian voice for space, land where man stands alone as an abstract being who would have to recommence the history of the species—or to conclude it.

Martinez Estrada, "Los Señores de la Nada"

Yearning plain, dematerialized;

Metaphysical peace. Divine geometry

Of abstract horizons and stripped land.

Landscape of the space, dreams of the firmament

Glory of solitude in savage ambits

Mane, wings, and clouds for the winds' joy.

Larreta, "La Pampa"

RIVER

First he was believed to be a sea: the sweet sea; now we know that he is the estuary where two rivers come

together. Tomorrow, it will be said that he is still the Pampa that here becomes water, in the same manner

as in other parts he becomes roofs or sky.

Martinez Estrada, Cabeza de Goliath

Other beautiful rivers

have beautiful colors...

Other, are deeper,

other, bluer, run

along delicate gardens

and magnificent forests.

You, sea of dark waters,

wide pampa of copper,

give distance

to man's daydream...

You, Rio de la Plata,

have the horizon.

Yunque, "Loa al Rio de la Plata"

TWILIGHT

The hour of Buenos Aires is the

afternoon, the hour of the desert. It is

then when the city acquires her

cosmical aura.

Twilight of the dove

Did the Hebrews call the beginning of afternoon . . .

In that hour of fine sandy light,

My roaming met with an unknown street,

Open with the noble ampleness of a terrace

And revealing on cornices and walls

Colors as soft as that same sky

That stirred in the background.

. . . and the environs of the twilight!

Gigantic sunsets occur exalting the

depth of the streets, scarcely contained

by the sky. To have our eyes whipped

by the sunsets' rigorous passion we

must resort to the outskirts which

oppose both "pampas."

Faced with the metropolis' indecision,

the houses at its edge assume a

challenging role in front of that

absolute horizontal, where the sunsets

promenade grandiosely like wandering

steamers.

Borges, "Fervor de Buenos Aires"

The Memorable Horizontal

All at once, above the first illuminated beacons, I saw Buenos Aires. The uniform river, flat, without limits to the left and to right; above your Argentine sky so filled with stars; a Buenos Aires, this phenomenal line of light beginning on the right at infinite and fleeing to the left toward infinity. Nothing else, except, at the center of the line of light, the electric glitter which announces the heart of the city. The simple meeting of the Pampas and the river in one line, illuminated the night from one end to the other.

Mirage, miracle of the night, the simple punctuation regular and infinite of the lights of the city describes what Buenos Aires is in the eyes of the voyageur. This vision remained for one intense and imperious I thought: nothing exists in Buenos Aires; but what a strong and majestic line.

Le Corbusier, *Précisions*

Roofs

London and New York are metropolises symbolic of two islands. Buenos Aires has been engendered and conceived by the plain. Horizontal surface: this is the key word. New York is all facades. Buenos Aires is all roofs. From the sky New York is a honeycomb of masonry icicles. Buenos Aires is plains and sky. In the same manner as one has to see the Pampa from below because it continues until it fuses with the firmament (and it can be said that it is more sky than land), one has to see the city from 1,500 kilometers high (for the real facade of Buenos Aires is her roofs).

The city is an immense roof, carefully gridded, as if it were a pavement. A floor was laid over the earth, on top of this another, and thus the land gets built resembling the layers of pampean earth.

Martinez Estrada, "Desde el Cielo"

Streets

Buenos Aires is the faithful image of the great plain that, encircling her, has its straightness continued in the rectitude of the streets and houses. The horizontal lines overcome the vertical. The perspectives—of one and two storey dwellings lined up and facing one another for miles and miles of asphalt and stone—are too easy to be believed. Each crossroad intersected by four infinites.

Borges, "Las Calles"

Streets of Buenos Aires, designed for the long vista, all the way to the horizon. Through those straight infinite streets, along those gutters, the country empties into the cities, the cities empty into Buenos Aires, and all of them empty into the river.

Martinez Estrada, "Pampa y Techos"

PLAZAS

I want to talk about the plazas. In Buenos Aires the plazas—noble pools overstocked with freshness, congresses of patrician trees, stages for romantic rendezvous—are the stillwaters where the streets resign their persistent geometrical flow, break formation, and joyously disperse.

Borges, "Plazas"

PATIO

With the evening

the two or three colors of the patio grew weary.

The huge candour of the full moon

no longer enchants her habitual firmament.

Patio, channel of sky.

The patio is the window

through which god watches souls.

The patio is the slope

down which the sky flows into the house.

Serene.

Eternity waits at the crossroads of stars.

How beautiful to live in friendship with the shade

of a porch, eaves, and a well.

Borges, "Patio"

IDEAL CITY

The man of the interior has stripped Buenos Aires of any materiality and transformed her into a formidable emporium of the best that exists in our reality and in our imagination. Thus, Buenos Aires is the center of a circumference formed by the most populated points and cultivated by the interior. They are all at the same distance. They are periphery as she is center. As in Borges' "Pascal," where nature is space, Buenos Aires remained "an infinite sphere with a center in all parts and a circumference nowhere."

She is a kind of "civic divinity," the federal district that twenty-one provinces have envisioned as the other city; the other life; the certainty of greatness; "the ideal city."

Martinez Estrada, "Civitas"

MANHATTAN: CAPITAL OF THE XXTH CENTURY
1969

"once I have grasped it, then an old, as it were rebellious, half apocalyptic province

of my thoughts will have been subdued, colonized, set in order."

Walter Benjamin, *in a Letter to Gerhard Scholem*

Manhattan, unencumbered by permanent memory, and more interested in becoming than in being, can be seen as the city of that second technological revolution brought about by the development of processes for producing and controlling information rather than just energy. It has, after all, incorporated the worship of communication with the idolatry of the industrial product and, by so doing, provided the ground for supporting any infatuation with now-as-the-ultimate configuration of reality. However, seen in a different light, Manhattan may reveal an unforeseen potential for conceiving of a quite different notion of city.

Manhattan is, in essence, a network. If beheld as an infrastructure for the processing and exchange of matter, energy, and information. Manhattan may be seen either as the overwrought roof of a subterranean physical grid of subway tunnels and train stations, automobile passages, postal tubes, sewage chambers, water and gas pipes, power wires, telephone, telegraph, television and computer lines; or, conversely, as the datum plane of an aerial lattice of flight patterns, wireless impulses, institutional liaisons, and ideological webs. In any of these roles, the points of interaction within Manhattan's network have been repeatedly charged, on and off, with different meanings. Entire systems and isolated elements have been connected to and processed by these networks, only to be later removed and replaced by new ones.

Were we willing, for the sake of argument, to suspend disbelief, forget coordinates, and imagine that all present structures have been completely removed, Manhattan's infrastructure would emerge — in all the complexity of its physical organization, the capacity of its input-output mechanism, and the versatility of its control devices — as the most representative urban artifact of our culture.

Freed in this manner from its current limitations, we may, to further this transfer operation, remove Manhattan's infrastructure from its present context and place it in the center of San Francisco Bay, on the plains of Africa, among the chateaux of the Loire Valley, or along the Wall of China . . .

Manhattan's infrastructure, thus liberated, belongs to all. But an infrastructure, though necessary, is not sufficient to make a city. The next step is, then, for all to undertake the postulation of its possible structures. The methods may belong either to remembrance or to invention, for, conceived as the idea rather than as the actual configuration, Manhattan's infrastructure provides the framework in which all crystallized fragments rescued from the city of the memory, and all figments envisioned for the city of the imagination, may dwell in ensemble, if not by reason of their casual relationships (since no reconstruction is hereby intended), then by grace of their affinities. The outcome of such undertaking may be agitational, and render, if not actual proposals of structures, at least an explicit Inventory of Qualities of urban existence toward a yet to be defined "City of Open Presents."

In a first, retrospective phase, we may, as one of many possible approaches, assemble in a piecemeal manner any surviving fragments of the memory on the infrastructure:

Bologna's arcades, Osip Mandelstam's St. Petersburg, John Nash's Regent's Park, Gabriel's Petit Trianon, Katsura's promenades to observe the sunset, Mies' Barcelona Pavilion, Wallace Stevens' wind on a wheatfield, John Soane's house, Frank Zappa's Los Angeles, Baudelaire's fleeting instants, Debussy's submerged cathedral, Michael Heizer's land marks, Joan Littlewood's fun palace, Ray Bradbury's brown clouds, Le Notre's Gardens of Chantilly . . .

In a second, prospective phase, the form of any structure to be assembled on the infrastructure is to come from the domain of invention.

But envisioned qualities do not come in wholes. They are to be apprehended as they rush by — partial denotators of an inversed tradition, of possible states which may become; and once grasped, they are to be dialectically confronted with the many meanings that can be temporarily assigned to our fragmentary experiences of the Present.

As the meanings of these structures can only be interpreted in the context of the relationships they establish with other structures, this process would generate new meanings which in turn would require further interpretation. It is by this reiterative process that the envisioned structures would assume constructive powers. Insofar as they would question the context of the Present, they would assign it new meanings; insofar as they would propose alternative states, they would re-structure it.

This tearing of the fragment from its former context, this rescuing of the irreducible word from its decayed sentence, involves not only the usual process of design by discriminate selection but suggests, moreover, a process of bringing together where, instead of establishing fixed hierarchies, the fragments rescued from tradition are placed on the same level in ever changing contiguities, in order to yield new meanings, and thereby render other modes of access to their recondite qualities.

THE UNIVERCITY
1972

To culminate his long tenure in a fitting manner, the Governor of the North-Eastern Region conceived of creating a new city. Intent on minimizing the political and financial struggles which in the past had invariably deformed the destiny of other cities, he proposed that the new city be designed and managed by the University of the North-Eastern Region.

This University had been established more than a century ago, to contribute solutions to the problems of an evolving rural society. Having fulfilled its task with a modicum of accomplishment, the University was, nevertheless, becoming increasingly aware that the main areas of intellectual speculation and artistic imagery had been shifting from an anxious observation of the natural milieu to an anguished inquiry into the nature and praxis of the man-made environment. The Governor's intentions suited the University's need for intellectual expansion, and the proposed task was accepted.

The new city was to be the University's laboratory for urban and institutional innovations — preventive health care, personal and mass transportation systems, different forms of neighborhood government and communal living, new working and leisure patterns — these were just a few of the ideas the University intended to test there.

The Grant Act which once had sponsored the creation of the original University was unearthed. By carefully stretching some of its original meaning, the Regional Legislature granted the University large extensions of public land. The University's financial arm — the Bank of Univercity, as the city was to become known — issued bonds on this land to finance construction. To avoid land speculation, Univercity and its surrounding countryside were to remain the property of the North-Eastern University. Land for industrial use could only be leased, while, to further experimentation in social groupings, housing leases would be signed not by a family, but by each of its members as individuals.

Another branch of the University, its Urban Planning and Development Institute, was put in charge of designing the city, supervising its construction, and managing the new city's infrastructural services. It was also to supervise some of its superstructural aspects, especially those pertaining to educational, cultural and leisure activities.

The new city's physical plan was to be based on the concept of open-ended systems. It was to provide an urban system capable of interacting with its surrounding context, and of receiving new or removing old sub-systems without unduly affecting the rest of the city's processes. The technicians of the interdisciplinary design team hoped that the city resulting from such a dynamic model would foster the maximum of social communication.

A varied and representative cross section of the Region's population willingly settled there, once Univercity's concepts and goals became known. In a few years, the population became stabilized at 100,000 inhabitants and, in a relatively short time, it became the much talked-about showcase its founders had hoped for. Naturally, in its first stages, Univercity underwent the normal adjustment problems, but on the whole it prospered as had been projected.

As time passed by, however, an indefinable yet perceptible shift in Univercity's goals and behaviors began to take place. No one has yet been able to establish exactly in what manner and why, but it is suspected that some of the experiments on which Univercity was based got out of control, generating totally unexpected secondary and tertiary consequences.

It would seem that the beginnings of the change were subtle and, in turn, gentle. It is assumed that it all began when, in opposite corners of the city, altars to Revolution and Redemption were built. Although no one actually believed in gods, playing off the divinities against the other was perhaps a useful device for gaining terrain for their own human goals.

Later, the citizens established a cemetery in the center of the city. The Future was buried there several times, only to be exhumed periodically by a few who felt they could not go on without its forwarding image. In another part of the city, members of a much different group devoted themselves to exorcising the guilt of history by making collective gestures endowed with the power to obliterate individual memories, they believed. These seem to have been the same who decided their newborn babies should be considered 120 years old. It is surmised that they did so not so much hoping that the ever-present knowledge of the end would prevent their engaging in harsh longings or the pursuit of vainglory, but, rather, wanting their children to grow up with the awareness that any wager against mortality was an insane challenge.

As generations changed, uncertainty, which in olden times used to dress itself up as language, gave way to purposeful silence. Music and mathematics became Univercity's form of mystical experience and epistemological transaction. Words, forgotten and aimless, roamed the city, gradually returning to the chaos to which they had once belonged.

On festive occasions, the days blended into the nights as the inhabitants gathered to promenade their feelings and dance their passions. The rest of the time they remained in the quietude of their places, making objects or turning thoughts. With these creations, they hoped to reconcile their desire with their fears. It was felt that the power of these creations depended on their meaning not becoming known until they had become form, and the most powerful constructs were assumed to be those which remained closed up in their recondite condition until ready to reveal themselves. Stones and water — and all examples of real and imagined creation — were revered as inner forms which had not yet revealed their signs.

Those without a gift for numbers and deaf to sound dedicated themselves to architecture. At one end of town they delineated a parcel of land in the almond shape of an eye, digging until water level was reached. With the earth that had been removed, they built a square platform at the opposite end of town. On it they drew an orthogonal grid, building at every crossing square towers ten steps wide and one hundred steps high. The first tower was made of sandstone and the last of ice, but all seemed to be of the same material, so subtle was the series and so large the number.

At this point, however, even conjecture must stop, for none can claim to know how or why Univercity disappeared. It might have been possible to surmise some of the changes that took place in Univercity by observing transformations that also occurred around that time in some of the neighboring cities that survived the disappearance of Univercity; but this task would have been hindered by the fact that almost all records of the history of Univercity itself have literally vanished.

Numberless hypotheses are brought up about the end of Univercity. There are those who maintain that the Regional Government at first tolerated the unexpected turns Univercity had been taking, rationalizing it a a useful experiment which they could well afford, as long as it remained circumscribed. But later, as its influence began to pervade the ways of perceiving and acting upon reality of the people of other cities in the Region, the Government decided that it was imperative to bring Univercity to a fast and thorough end.

The speculative variaitons on the possible reasoning behind such a decision are immeasurable. While some maintain that it came about because Univercity taught a subversive alternative to the prevailing conditions, others believe that it was becoming increasingly evident to the people of the region that Univercity could only remain the exemplary model as long as they were willing to continue toiling to maintain an ideal they themselves could never hope to become.

Whenever a few of us risk gathering in secret to evoke its unbearable absence, we quietly tell each other that Univercity is still somewhere in the Region, transparent and silent by its own will. For us, Univercity is still here, waiting for none, but willing to be turned once more into a fable by the passing shadow of those who may unite for a perfect instant to bring its image to light.

La Città del Design
1973

Italy has remained a federation of city-states. There are museum-cities and factory-cities. There is a city whose streets are made of water, and another where all streets are hollowed walls. There is one city where all its inhabitants work on the manufacture of equipment for amusement parks; a second where everybody makes shoes; and a third where all its dwellers build baroque furniture. There are many cities where they still make a living by baking bread and bottling wine, and one where they continue to package faith and transact with guilt. Naturally, there is also one city inhabited solely by architects and designers. This city is laid out on a grid, its blocks are square, and each is totally occupied by a cubic building. Its walls are blind, without windows or doors.

The inhabitants of this city pride themselves on being radically different from each other. Visitors to the city claim, however, that all inhabitants have one common trait; they are all unhappy with the city they inherited and moreover, concur that it is possible to divide the citizens into several distinct groups.

The members of one of the groups live inside the building blocks. Conscious of the impossibility of communicating with others, each of them, in the isolation of of his own block, builds and demolishes every day, a new physical setting. To these constructions they sometimes give forms which they recover from their private memories; on other occasions, these constructs are intended to represent what they envision communal life may be on the outside.

Another group dwells in the streets. Both as individuals or as members of often conflicting sub-groups, they have one common goal: to destroy the blocks that define the streets. For that purpose they march along chanting invocations, or write on the walls words and symbols which they believe are endowed with the power to bring about their will.

There is one group whose members sit on top of the buildings. There they await the emergence of the first blade of grass from the roof that will announce the arrival of the Millennium.

As of late, rumors have been circulating that some members of the group dwelling in the streets have climbed up to the buildings' roof-tops, hoping that from this vantage point they could be able to see whether the legendary people of the countryside have begun their much predicted march against the city, or whether they have opted to build a new city beyond the boundaries of the old one.

A very large American company came to us, interested in investing some of their assets outside their traditional area of activity. Specifically, they wanted to invest in housing, and asked us to develop designs and a development program with a view toward establishing a factory for producing prefabricated houses. Ample research and development funds were allocated and a professional fee was agreed upon. We accepted the commission.

The first step was to create a Catalog of Domestic Places, organized into two sections: retrospective and prospective.

The retrospective section was conceived as an operation of the memory; an historical collection of places of the house, those fragments that had survived the evanescence of their original context: Pompeian atriums; Japanese terraces to observe the sunset; ambulatories, patios, and courtyards; medieval window seats; Roman baths; roof gardens; arcaded porches, foyers, and entrance halls . . .

The prospective section was intended as an exercise of the imagination, and involved designing places with no historical antecedents. It postulated new spatial concepts which corresponded to emerging notions of flexibility and adaptability, territoriality, and individual privacy.

Each of these places — those recovered as well as those postulated — was printed on a double page spread in the Catalog. On the left hand page were indicated plans, sections, and elevations; on the right hand page was an axonometric drawing of the place. In the retrospective section, whenever possible, photos were added which were slightly blurred so as not to fully reveal texture while still denoting mass and space.

Once the Catalog was completed we proceeded to the experimental stage. The goal was to test the capability of the proposed housing method to satisfy the housing needs not only of a large number of users of similar socio-economic background, but also the diverse housing requirements of small groups representing different backgrounds. For this testing phase we searched, and found, fourteen Californian families interested in developing jointly a housing project, and a piece of land was purchased there.

Each family was given a copy of the Catalog of Domestic Places, and the members of each family were asked to select those places they would like to have in their new homes. Once a family had completed its preliminary selection it would then sit down to discuss its choices with an architect member of the experimental design team. His task was to encourage the family to bring into a coherent scheme those elements it had selected. Thus, places were added that had been overlooked, while others were removed when it became clear that they were not as desirable as had first been thought. The combinations obtained were sometimes bizarre, but the experimental design team did its best to help each family achieve a scheme that satisfied the programmatic and social requirements of the family, as well as the psychological needs of every one of its members. The next step was for all families to design together a common space for socializing, sporting games, and child care. This was achieved, but not without some tensions and conflicts flaring up here and there.

The experimental design team elaborated each family's scheme, producing diagrammatic plans, sections, and elevations. Each dwelling was then given out for bids, and subcontracted to builders of the area. They were given neither working nor detail drawings, since these were to be solved by each contractor according to his own building techniques and available materials.

Construction proceeded as smoothly as could be expected with fourteen different owners looking over the contractor's shoulder, but the builders managed to produce the houses in time and more or less within the budget. True, the "Pompeian atriums," "Dutch gardens," and "Corbusian roof-gardens" lost some of their texture when translated into the California building vernacular, but the spaces were there alright. Although the juxtaposition of fragments recovered from different historical periods sometimes generated unintended ironies, they, nevertheless, also suggested new meanings.

Very importantly, the cost per square foot for each house was about the same as the most inexpensive prefabricated system, a system very rigid in comparison to ours. We felt we had managed to demonstrate to our satisfaction that a differentiated and participatory approach to industrialized housing was possible. But, since this approach did not require new factories, nor were new investments necessary, we were fired.

Designer/Producer
1971

A young man went to an industrialist and told him: "I am a designer who can make your products more beautiful and useful so you will sell more." The manufacturer laughed, "Silly boy," he thought, "doesn't he know about the powers of persuasion publicity already provides?" He went to another industrialist and told him: "I am a problem-solving designer. I can avoid production problems by designing better conceived products. I propose more efficient uses of your manufacturing resources and distribution capacity." "That sounds interesting, come in." The industrialist's engineers met him, but after 10 minutes they could hardly contain their sneering smiles. "Sad case," they thought. "Hasn't he yet realized the poverty of the intellectual and methodological equipment he was provided with at design school?

"What is a designer to do," he asked himself. "Didn't Gropius promise," he seemed to remember, "that a talented and ethical designer would inexorably find an enlightened industrialist, and that together they would create products the people would hail approvingly, recognizing in them their own zeitgeist justly expressed? It has not been true at all," he concluded. "Many facts upsetting the purity of design's ideology have been swept under history's rug."

"Didn't Hector Guimard own an iron foundry? And as for the Paris Metro entrance competition, the well-priced kilo rather than the gracefully turned line must have been the decisive fact in the mind of the judges," he ruefully surmised. "Was not Rietveld able to engage in formal exercises leading to his neo-plastic chair constructions because he had inherited a carpentry shop? Wasn't Breuer the partner of a drunkard who owned a tube-bending machine?" He was uncertain about the latter, but about Michael Thonet he was positive. "He was able to produce his splendid inventions because Prince Metternich granted him patent protections, in addition to financial backing for large-scale fabrication. No wonder he was able to build his designs."

"And what about Ford, Bugatti, Pinin Farina, Sikorsky, Schlumbohn and the others? What about the history of architecture? Wasn't it filled with similar cases: Nash, Eiffel, Adam, Nervi, and now, Portman? The great misfortune," he realized, "came about when the designer acquiesced to specialized and compartmentalized knowledge, accepting the established relationships of production in exchange for the protection of managers and captains of industry."

What was he to do? Turn the clock back 10 years and go to a country where industrialization was just beginning? Design a plexiglass cover for cookbooks that he could produce himself in his garage? Cottage industry, he felt, was an honorable alternative but only satisfactory as long as it concerned itself with producing small-scale simple objects.

He had conceived a mechanically advanced chair to be used by convalescents and the elderly at home. Should he publish the idea? It would raise the designers' level of consciousness which, he presumed, was already quite high, but would certainly not move the hearts of the manufacturers.

He considered applying for research and development funds from Government agencies, but he recoiled in horror, imagining himself five years later roaming governmental offices, pushing one application form after the next. He was convinced that it was useless to try to interest a manufacturer; most of them would not care to produce something for a small, specialized market. A few might take on the project, but would prolong the development phase for as long as it allowed them to publicly wash away their social guilt. A handful might take it on sincerely; but, even with the best of intentions, the project would be given low priority and might never be produced.

Discouragement took hold of him. He found strength, though, in his belief, perhaps naive but very passionate, that he had a moral responsibility to bring his idea into existence. He decided that design, development, and the capacity to build the production tools, if not the product itself, had to be reunited.

He visited several craftsmen he knew: a wood model-maker, three industrial mechanics, a mold-maker, a retired production manager, and two people who once helped him sand-cast an aluminium piece. He found them all, in one way or another, dissatisfied with the practice of their crafts. The old mold-maker was the most difficult case. Having grown fond of gardening, he despaired that his art could ever equal the marvel of seeds which follow no matrix to arrive at their form. Others, like the wood model-maker and the mechanics, growing increasingly despondent, told only their specific task, rarely knew what role their efforts played in the overall design.

He proposed that they form a cooperative. "Together," he said, "we shall make a list of things that we believe people, such as children, factory workers, the elderly, really need but cannot obtain." He added that they would naturally tackle only those problems within their reach. He convinced them that if they needed outside advice, from doctors or engineers, they would find sympathetic cooperation. His own task was to define problems and propose design solutions. If, after discussion, the group agreed to undertake the project, the model-maker and the mechanic would build the prototypes to be tested; the production engineer would suggest manufacturing methods, and the mold-maker would make the dies. Any other necessary skills would be found among their friends.

After a great deal of deliberation, they decided to join forces. Their hopes for success rested on the strength of their combined skills more than their limited funds. Their plan was as follows: once a prototype had been built, tested and jointly approved, they would build the molds, the dies, and even the machines needed to produce their designs. When the production equipment was complete, they would approach a manufacturer. Since, at that stage, they would already have assumed most of the risks, they were hopeful no manufacturer could refuse them, even if the product was a paraplegic's chair or a set of knives and forks to be used by people with arthritis. To give themselves courage, they told each other that if they failed to find a manufacturer, there was nothing to prevent them manufacturing the design themselves. Obviously, distribution would not be an easy task, but they hoped to find outlets for whatever they were capable of producing.

The following years proved more difficult than they had expected. Slowly but unremittingly, their creations developed: stools so designed that a worker on an assembly-line could unload his weight on three rather than on two legs; a bio-engineered leg-sleeve designed to aid the blood circulation of workers who had to stand all day; an office chair especially designed to match the different postures a seated person adopts at work; a set of long-grip pliers for wheelchair-bound people to reach distant objects.

Money was scarce, but they had the ineffable pleasure of seeing their products used by those who needed them. The reputation of the co-operative and its products grew; young designers came from far to offer their services. But the answer they received at the door was always the same one: "You are an industrial designer? So sorry, so sorry, we have no use for them. Now, if you were a cosmologist . . ."

CODA: A PRE-DESIGN CONDITION
1968

Distrustful of deterministic models and the 19th Century concept of change; repelled by the impermeability of Europe's political and educational institutions yet simultaneously resisting the sponginess of America's cultural and social establishment; Youth—self assured of purity by its refusal to define plans and buoyed by the tension of its own contradictions—envisions, nevertheless, an undeterministic type of social system, tolerant of emotions and designed to operate in a permanent state of reform.

The disruption of classes in Nanterre's New Faculty of Letters led by Daniel Cohn-Bendit, the supporting student demonstrations in Paris, the police invasion of the Sorbonne, the occupation of the Sorbonne and the Odeon by the students, the first and second barricades, and the government's reaction and referendum are by now well-known items for a yet unconcluded chronology of youth's rebellion. But, in contrast to the manifestos of revolution, which have always been rooted in the future, the propaganda of the French revolt nourished itself in immediacy.

Graffiti sustained a relentless match of squash against the communiques of the official radio and TV. Slogans were picked off the walls and brought to the limited printing facilities of L'Ecole des Arts Decoratifs and L'Ecole de Beaux-Arts, rebaptized Atelier Populaire by the students entrenched there. Students and sympathetic workers enraptured by the spirit of community experimented with participatory design, discussing and choosing together the poster subjects and images. Anonymity was not only a consequence of this method of working but also an understandable necessity.

The first posters were printed by whatever means were at hand. As the movement became more organized and the number of those involved increased, silk screen workshops were established. When need overcame production, the ateliers were joined by the workshops of the Faculties of Science and of Psychology, as well as by the Committees of Revolutionary Action operating in each neighborhood which resorted to every available printing medium—blue print and office duplicating machines included.

Resorting to the folklore of popular idioms and visual images was the students' way of achieving more directly the desired union of university and factory. Nevertheless, it gradually became clear that Tomorrow had many forms of commitment to reality. While the students had been proposing humanistic anarchism as natural man's Garden, the majority of the workers had been demanding the Arcadia of the Levittowns. But then, Today understood will be the myth of history and these posters, its documents. For its actors, the reality of May dwells in the paper barricade and in the fervid hours of their collective creation.

1. The realm of ideas and the material realm come together and interact at the level of structures. A structure attempts to materialize an idea and to idealize a material. It is designed to reconcile the discordant interface between superstructure and infrastructure, and it may bring about changes in both by the properties inherent in its particular formal organization, through the particular instabilities which are likely to follow its attempted resolution of the conflicts between the two realms. A structure may act as a pattern-breaker, it may dissolve established correspondences between thought and matter and introduce new ones; it may induce a physical rearrangement in the infrastructure and an epistemological renewal at the level of the superstructure.

2. Man creates structures that establish a meeting ground between two incommeasurable realms. In a phenomenological view, his material being—himself, his production and reproduction—is his main concern in creating structures. These formal organizations are then to legitimize social relations, the ownership of resources, etc. According to an existential view, the structures that man designs, the myths he creates, are temporary crystallizations in the perennial state of dialectical transaction between the fears and desires underlying the individual's aspirations and the assembled forces of the natural and socio-cultural worlds.

3. It has been argued that technology in advanced industrial society—of the East as well as the West—has become a kind of ideology which legitimizes present forms of managerial authority by setting up production and consumption, the means and products of technology, as desirable ends in themselves. Traditional distinctions between infrastructure and superstructure have gotten blurred.

    It is the contradictions between infrastructure and superstructure that are the source of such problems as alienation, the curtailment of freedom, and fragmentation of knowledge. And these problems, in spite of the blurring of the traditional distinctions between the two levels, are still very much with us.

4. The now-vacant stead of the traditional agent of change, the class-subject, is spottily assumed by a lucid and sensitive few who place themselves on the periphery of the system. They may attempt to establish alliances with those who are dispossessed or deprived of their rights, but these are now outside channels of production and wield no power; and the alienated ones who do take part in production can no longer recognize themselves as a social class. Contestation is then reduced to an act of the private consciousness, done in despair because it knows itself powerless. Subjective contestation has so far adopted two main forms. Some advocate abstention from practice—"moratorium" as a strategy; for others violence becomes the surrogate for a notion of praxis now exhausted of its traditional meaning.

5. Class structure having lost its meaning in an advanced industrial situation, how can a society of individuals implement change? First, it has to be recognized, that, even though the old distinctions have been blurred, conflicts, albeit of a different nature, still exist between infrastructure and superstructure. The strategy that is called for is the design of structures which, mediating between the two levels, attempt to resolve their new kinds of conflict, and to cause in both changes that are wanted.

    What these structures can and ought to be cannot be known in advance of their existence. However, as we have seen, in an advanced industrial society the conditions do not exist which permit the emergence of structures that may bring about significant change.

    We are, so to speak, in a pre-design situation. A special kind of structure has to be provided in the first place that will channel and make effective the opposition of those who are dissatisfied with the state of things. That is to say, a prior structure is needed to permit the design of new structures.

    Conflicts may sometimes be solved by an unstructured situation rather than a new structure; in that case it is the context that has to be designed to permit the unstructured situation to exist.

6. The functions that are necessary for change already exist in the present structures of society. These are the mediating functions (informational, decision-making, regulatory, etc.) whereby the infrastructure and the superstructure are connected and their conflicts negotiated. What is needed is that they be repossessed and given a new social structure. If this is to be the special kind of pre-design organization that would provide the context for the design of new structures it should satisfy a number of conditions. Its internal organization should be open-ended, capable of constant rearrangement to accommodate the new structures that arise. It should not only foster the proposals of individuals but also be able to contribute toward their implementation. It should deal not only with material but especially with epistemological production. Its indeterministic nature demands the development, and the constant reexamination of an explicit system of ethics to guide the design of the new structures it will help bring about. In the past, when conflicts were more clearly defined along class lines, courses of action that could be taken to bring about change were more narrowly determined; whereas the pre-design structure that we contemplate would make action possible in a less determined situation, offering a broader choice of alternatives that exist as real possibilities, and giving individuals more power to influence historical development. This social ethics should be based on the needs and aspirations of individuals. The child of an ethical decision, this pre-design structure should itself be the matrix of ethical decisions.

ARCHITECTURE

SAN ANTONIO BOTANICAL CENTER—LUCILLE HALSELL CONSERVATORY

CENTER FOR APPLIED COMPUTER RESEARCH

GRAND RAPIDS ART MUSEUM

COOPERATIVE OF MEXICAN AMERICAN GRAPE GROWERS

BANQUE BRUXELLES LAMBERT, MILAN

MANOIR D'ANGOUSSART

MUSEUM OF AMERICAN FOLK ART

CASA DE RETIRO ESPIRITUAL

PRO MEMORIA GARDEN

BANQUE BRUXELLES LAMBERT, LAUSANNE

HOUSTON CENTER PLAZA

SCHLUMBERGER RESEARCH LABORATORIES

HOUSE FOR LEO CASTELLI

PLAZA MAYOR

BANQUE BRUXELLES LAMBERT, NEW YORK

ELECTIVE AFFINITIES

NEW ORLEANS MUSEUM OF ART

EMILIO'S FOLLY: MAN IS AN ISLAND

ESCHENHEIMER TOWER

FINANCIAL GUARANTY INSURANCE CORPORATION

MERCEDES BENZ SHOWROOM

RESIDENCE-AU-LAC

MASTER PLAN FOR THE UNIVERSAL EXPOSITION—SEVILLA, 1992

FRANKFURT ZOO

NICHII OBIHIRO DEPARTMENT STORE

UNION STATION

LUCILLE HALSELL CONSERVATORY
SAN ANTONIO, TEXAS

The Lucille Halsell Conservatory is a complex of greenhouses located in the hot, dry climate of southern Texas. Unlike northern climates, where traditionally glazed greenhouses maximize sunlight, the climate of San Antonio requires that plants be shielded from the sun.

This proposal uses the earth as a container and protector of the plants, controlling light and heat levels by limiting glazed areas to the roof. Since it is sheltered by earth berms, the conservatory preserves and harmonizes with the gently rolling hills around it. While the glazing is used as a cover for the earthen container, the roof is raised in places to accommodate tall plants. The varied forms of these peaks take advantage of prevailing conditions and orientation to the sun, and give the roofs a hieratic presence as an arrangement of secular temples sitting serenely in the landscape.

The different rooms within the center are organized around a garden patio, or courtyard, typical of Texas vernacular architecture, affording access to the different greenhouses under a shaded arcade, unifying the various buildings. Each room can thus be treated as a separate building, with its own special climatic conditions and spatial configuration. This imparts a processional quality to the sequence of circulation through the conservatory: the entrance pavilion with a symbolic tree; the long, narrow orangery lined with fruit trees; the peaceful fern room with its water cascades and mists; and the rooms with special environments. This procession culminates in the grand palm court where a ramp wraps around the forest of trees, allowing people to move smoothly to the roof where they can view the plants from above, thus transforming a theoretically small construction into a structure of much grander scale.

The project provides a unique architectural solution to the problem of designing a greenhouse in a hot, dry climate. While recognizing regional vernacular in organizing the buildings around a courtyard with a shaded arcade, the treatment of the earth as a container and glazing as merely a cover with additional peaks reduce the amount of sunlight. This allows the complex to harmonize with its surroundings and enhances it with sculptural objects.

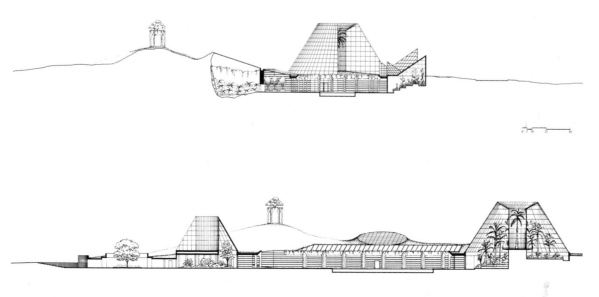

CENTER FOR APPLIED COMPUTER RESEARCH
MEXICO CITY, MEXICO

The Center for Applied Computer Research and Programming (Centro Mexicano de Calculo Aplicado S.A.) is a semi-public corporation that offers advanced computer programming services to public agencies and private organizations. Its headquarters will be the first of a series of private and public office buildings to be developed on the grounds of the former ranch, "Las Promesas," on the outskirts of Mexico City. This building will, therefore, serve as a landmark establishing the development's primary reference point, and defining the site's southeast and southwest boundaries, along which all future buildings will stand.

Approximately 160 people will use the building, including mathematicians, economists, computer programmers, and support staff. These users require flexible work spaces that can be made larger or smaller, and reorganized according to the requirements of a specific project as well as the psychological need for territorial identity of the various project groups.

The site conditions suggested the solution to the need for flexibility. Because Mexico City and its surroundings are built on the land-filled site of an ancient lagoon, the building has a large (150 meters square) water basin which drains the soil and prevents foundation problems. To take full advantage of this basin, the building's office/workspaces have been designed as barges, which float until positioned in place. Their watertight compartments are then filled, and the barges come to rest on the bottom of the four foot deep basin. To reposition them, water is pumped out of the compartments and the barges are floated to new locations.

The premise behind the design of this flexible environment is that nobody should have to work. At worst, it should be possible to work at home, in which case the need would not be for a large building but for a relatively small one to house the computer and receive messages. The building has been conceived, therefore, as a set of elements that could be progressively removed as the users' preferences change and the need for on-site space diminishes. Ultimately, only the silent walls and a single barge, turned into an island of flowers, would remain.

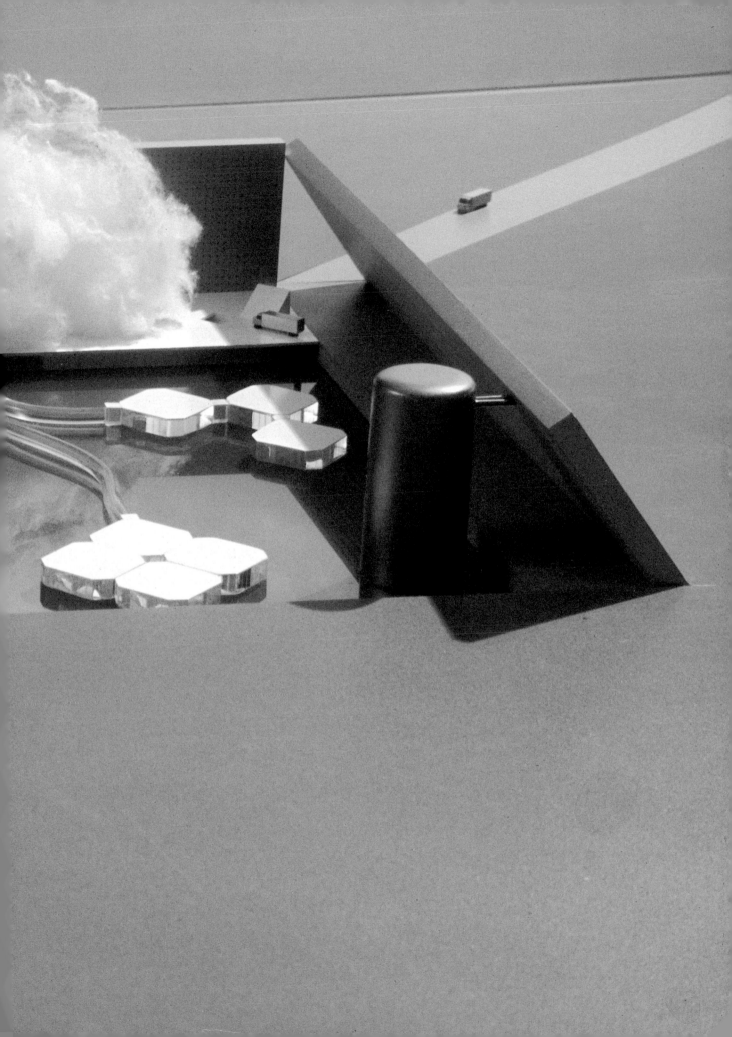

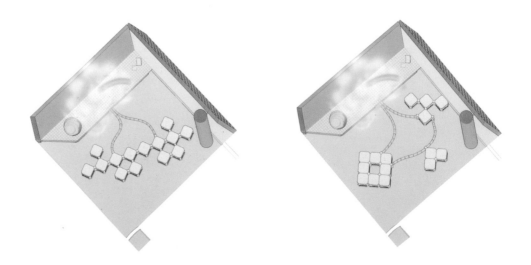

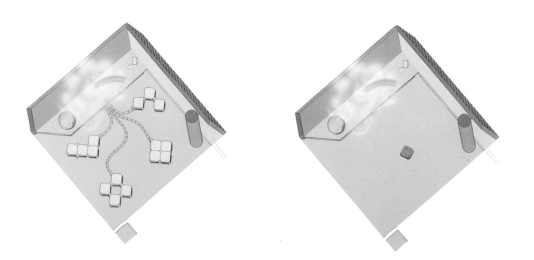

Grand Rapids Arts Museum
Grand Rapids, Michigan

This proposal, for the Grand Rapids Art Museum (GRAM) contributes to the revitalization of the downtown area in two ways: by reusing a distinguished but now vacant former government building as the GRAM's headquarters, and by addressing the possibility of using a number of neighboring buildings, which are also underused or abandoned, for functions that are compatible with the GRAM's cultural mission.

The 1908 Federal Building, a fine example of Beaux-Arts architecture, has served as the seat of public agencies, a courthouse, and, most recently, as a post office. The building will be upgraded to meet codes and programmatic requirements, and its exterior will be maintained as it is, with one important change: its entrance will be moved from the closed side of the U-shaped building to the open courtyard. This move establishes a direct physical relationship between the GRAM and a junior college whose students will be some of the GRAM's main users; it reorients the building toward Division Street, the important edge of downtown commercial redevelopment; and it provides a single, unified entrance for the various functions (museum, community spaces, artists' studios) that are housed in the building. These can all share the building's Grand Foyer, a ceremonial space that is created by covering the courtyard's open space with a translucent, inclined plane.

The inclined plane shields the courtyard, producing a gathering place and protecting the entrance to the museum. This plane also serves as a ceremonial stairway to the Grand Foyer, which is reached through an opening halfway up the plane. Water will descend slowly and evenly from the top of the stairway along a channel carved into the plane, leaving a clear path for those walking up the stairs. This silent cascade becomes the focal point of the city's newest public space.

The GRAM's inclined plane, its identifying symbol, will also serve as an architectural sign, identifying the other buildings recovered in the GRAM development project. For example, an abandoned movie house will be renovated, and the inclined plane that leans against it and protects its entrance will signal its use as a GRAM adjunct. The appearance and texture of the planes will vary from building to building and the sidewalks in front of the buildings that form this complex will be given a similar, distinctive texture.

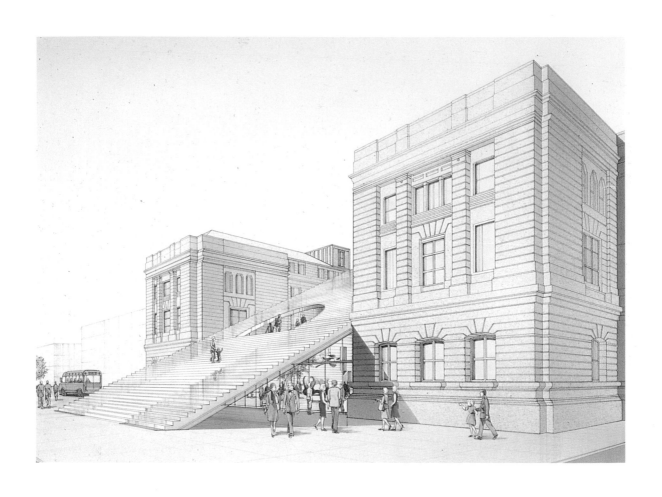

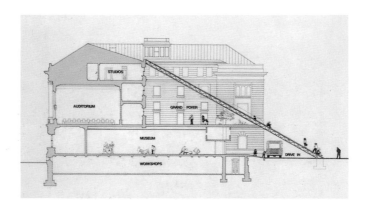

Cooperative of Mexican-American Grapegrowers
Borrego Springs, California

This project has been created at the request of a small cooperative of Mexican-American grape growers. The nine families that constitute the nucleus of this cooperative have, with the aid of federal and state grants and loans, been able to acquire land in a Southern California valley.

The climate there is warm and not ideal for grape growing. However, on the advice of viniculturists at the University of California, the farmers will employ a technique, used in Southern Europe, for growing grapes on an elevated grid of wires. The grid runs horizontally atop concrete or wooden columns ten foot high and 15 feet apart. The grapevines grow up, close to each column, and then branch out horizontally, supported by the wire grid. The grape leaves create a dense roof that shades the grapes from the sun, and also leaves the shaded ground free for the cultivation of other crops, such as asparagus.

This project is designed for a four phase settlement process. In the first phase, the nine founding families will live directly under the vineyard, where they will move with the mobile homes they already own. The entrance to the vineyard will be defined by opening a passage at the corner of two walls of a long-abandoned adobe ranch. Out of respect for the settlers' cultural heritage, the nine families' square plots will be laid out in a formal pattern reminiscent of early Hispano-American town. Parallel walls of hedges, defining the access road that runs from the entrance gate to the housing settlement, are planted to express the first settlers' hopes that the cooperative will prosper and grow along this avenue.

A small open-air chapel will be excavated in a stepped section until the first water level is reached. The chapel's cross will emerge from the water, and be repositioned as the water level changes. Every Sunday, as the parishioners go to church, they will take a shovelful of excavated earth from one of the two mounds at the chapel's entrance and shovel it onto the second mound, until only one mound remains Then the cycle will begin again.

Electricity will be provided by a generator connected to a large wooden paddle wheel at a pond. An earthen aqueduct will carry water from the pond to the animals' pen, which is sited so that the prevailing winds carry animal odors away from the settlement.

In the second phase, 16 new families will come and also bring their own trailers with them. But the organization of the hedge walls that form these families' private territories will be somewhat different. Two large residential squares, one for each group of eight families, will define a triangular plaza where dances will take place on Friday nights, and where an open-air market will be held each Saturday to sell the cooperative's products to the inhabitants of the neighboring towns. Each of these two squares will be divided into nine smaller squares. The central square will be a playground for small children, while the teenagers can meet for dates in the garden created at the pond's edge. Prism-like hedge formations, each about six feet square and 20 feet high, will form this garden; their arrangement in a gridded pattern provides the only urban order in the valley's vastness. A succession of small, private spaces hollowed out of the hedges offers secluded places where one can find privacy or two friends can meet.

One of the smaller squares facing the triangular plaza will be semi-public space, with a brick oven for cooking and large tables for communal noontime meals. These tables also serve as benches for the lessons on Mexican heritage that children will receive, in addition to their regular schooling.

By the time the second group of settlers arrives, the cooperative's production will have increased sufficiently to permit the building of a winery, which will be located near the entrance. Grapes will be stored in a conical silo, a structure traditionally used in Mexico for warehousing produce. The winery itself will be underground, in order to keep the wooden vats cool.

It is hoped that in the third phase, the internal hedge walls separating each family's private territory will have been clipped away, and a more communal pattern of living will have developed.

The fourth phase stands as a metaphor for the eternal wish that all walls wither away, and that man will be able to live in peace under a vineyard's shade, and off of its generous grapes.

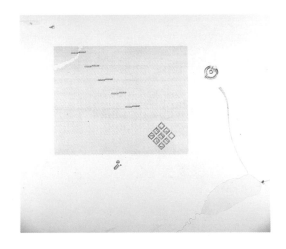

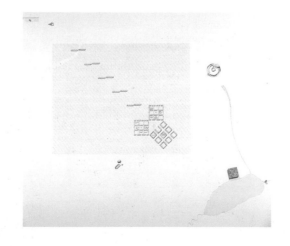

BANQUE BRUXELLES LAMBERT
MILAN, ITALY

The Milan branch of the Banque Bruxelles Lambert is housed in a 19th century building that had been decorated in high renaissance style on the ground floor, mannerist on the mezzanine, and which culminated in a grand roccoco hall of mirrors on the top floor. In renovating this building for use by the bank, the ornamental complex has been left intact but rigorously toned down, to create a subdued background (a sort of visual *basso continuo*) for the new bank. Accordingly, the rooms, with their newly-veiled ornament, were treated as "found sets," a series of ready-made stages that would enhance the new furniture selected for its architectural qualities—pure, minimalist volumes lacquered black to reflect in depth the rooms' ornament, and highly polished to emphasize their stereometry. These pieces, laid out to conform to the bank's functional requirements, serve as "architectural elements" in the "urban spaces" of the rooms.

In order to intensify the counterpoint between the new architectural design and the found setting, the simple but bold device of cordoning, or framing, the new areas with a conceptual black line was employed to help define the edges where new meets old. This black line appears in various forms: in the entrance's grand staircase, it is the curvilinear, free-flowing handrail; in the offices, it is expressed by straight black ribbons, about 7 centimeters wide, placed flat on the floor to frame the new installation.

This horizontal framing of new areas is further developed through the use of tall, slender, black floor lamps which define the vertical edges of the new areas. Although this three-dimensional framework was used consistently throughout the bank, each room was treated in a different manner befitting its use and its hierarchical position: in some cases the black ribbon traces the edges of a room, meeting the vertical element at the corners; in others, the points of the linear envelope are defined by the bases of the vertical lighting fixtures, while the black ribbon reflects only one half of the symmetrical floor design. In the two large working areas dedicated to credit and accounting, the black ribbons on the floor are made to bow in the center section to reflect a bay window, while on the opposite side of the room, freestanding containers are positioned to define a colonnade which suggests a functional corridor between two rooms. Using a few conceits of symmetry, each room is perceived as enclosed within, or enveloped by, a "prism" of edges.

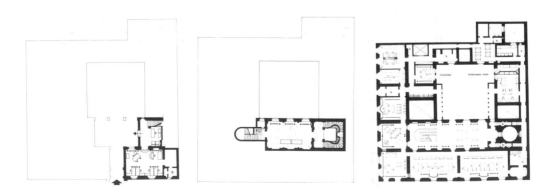

MANOIR D'ANGOUSSART
BIERGES, BELGIUM

This house and garden are conceived as a single, indivisible entity, while the diverse architectural elements that make up this 20-acre estate are treated as integral parts of the landscape. Contrary to the Palladian ideal of the villa—centripetal in organization and symmetrical in hierarchy—the Manoir d'Angoussart is centrifugal; its elements separated and disposed to suggest an expansive domain of ever-changing perspectives. Multiple secondary axes and vistas are intertwined, both with one another and with the main axis approaching the house.

Masses are defined by earth berms and by geometric volumes. Texture and ornament are provided by grass, plantings, and the moire patterns created by the window frames. The design is not only related to the earth, it is also rooted in the architectural tradition of the Low Countries. This is especially clear in the use of freestanding facades modulated by the orthogonal grid of a double layer of small window panes which are, in reality, a double lattice, which will be covered with ivy. A weather barrier is placed far behind the lattice facade which, when seen from afar, maintains a discreetly low profile. But as one approaches the house, the full height of the facade emerges, giving the house a majestic presence.

The design takes advantage of its site, which is completely flat except for a ravine facing south, by building the house into the earth, so that its largest windows open onto the ravine's view. Additional light enters through a generous central courtyard and a corner patio. The house is organized into three levels (playroom, living area, and sleeping area) around courtyards and cloisters. The use of earth as both shielding mass and container also insulates the house, insuring a pleasant temperature year-round. Moreover, the solar collectors placed on the south side of the swimming pool's berm will supply an array of photovoltaic panels that are sufficient in area, even at current low efficiencies, to satisfy the estate's energy needs.

The buildings on the estate will be constructed of two layers: an outer shell and an inner shall. The outer shell will be constructed of prefabricated, double-reinforced concrete panels, and treated as a "found structure," inside which interior furnishings and finishes are to be custom-fitted. The inner shell will be built in Italy, and reassembled inside the outer shell.

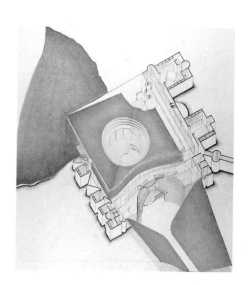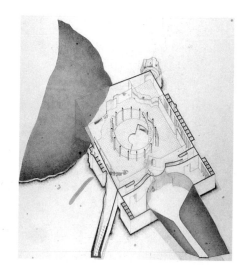

MUSEUM OF AMERICAN FOLK ART
NEW YORK CITY, NEW YORK

The Museum of American Folk Art, a relatively young institution that has won a scholarly reputation and wide national recognition, has operated until now from small, cramped quarters in midtown Manhattan. With both individual and foundation support, the museum has acquired a site on West 53rd Street near Sixth Avenue on which to build a new museum. In order to finance construction, the museum will use the site's air rights to build an office tower. The project requires, therefore, not only an art museum of architectural distinction, but a high-rise tower that contributes to New York's tall-building tradition. The design of the tower synthesizes the three major typologies of Manhattan skyscrapers: the "column" form of base, shaft, and capital that characterized the first high-rises of the 19th century; the "setback" building that resulted from the zoning regulations of the 1920's; and the glass prism, which made its debut in the 1940's with Le Corbusier's original designs for the United Nations.

The building is divided into three blocks of office floors that are suspended within a prismatic frame, or envelope. This geometric container relates the building to its neighbor on the west, and anticipates the shape of a planned building on its east side. The height of the base relates to the original Museum of Modern Art's roof line, and its tray corresponds to the heights of the 12 and 20-story buildings behind it. The tower reflects the visual primacy of Sixth Avenue and its corridor of tall buildings by staying lower than the maximum allowable building height.

The arrangement of the blocks reduces the tower's perceived mass, allows greater penetration of light through the building, and expresses the functions of its interior, while still presenting a unified face to the street. This visual organization allows a reading of the building in terms of the base, shaft, and capital of the old "column" typology. At the same time, by setting the blocks forward as they ascend, and expanding their horizontal span as their supporting piers grow taller and thinner, the design also recalls aspects of the setback building tradition. More importantly, these forward-stepping blocks focus attention on the building's main entrance portal. The freestanding 80 foot high portal, designed as a proscenium, provides a special identity for the museum while serving the office tower as well. The two asymmetrical stairways which penetrate the ceremonial entrance are deliberately monumental in feeling, and lead to the museum entrance and grand foyer, while the entrance to the tower is placed axially on the street level.

The museum entrance level houses ticket, information, and membership booths, a checkroom, and the first of the bookstore's two floors. The entrance level "opens up" onto a skylit, three-story, stepped-section inner court that is located in the rear of the museum. From the grand triangular staircase or the en-

trance-level parapet, visitors can look down onto two floors of exhibition space, as well as frontally toward quilts and large scale works displayed on the 25 foot high end wall. The grand foyer and entrance floor are a freestanding glass construction; the inclined plane of the outdoor sculpture area surrounding the lobby slants upward to emphasize the foyer's spatial detachment. From here visitors proceed down ramps or stairways to the exhibition floors, which are placed at half-levels. This arrangement orients and entices visitors, allowing them to look up or down to the two floors immediately above and below. The circulation pattern of these half-levels is designed as a central, elongated spiral, and the exhibition spaces at each level can be kept completely open, or subdivided into alcoves. These alcoves, which are domestic in scale to relate to the objects and paintings that constitute the museum's permanent collection, can be expanded into larger areas for temporary exhibitions.

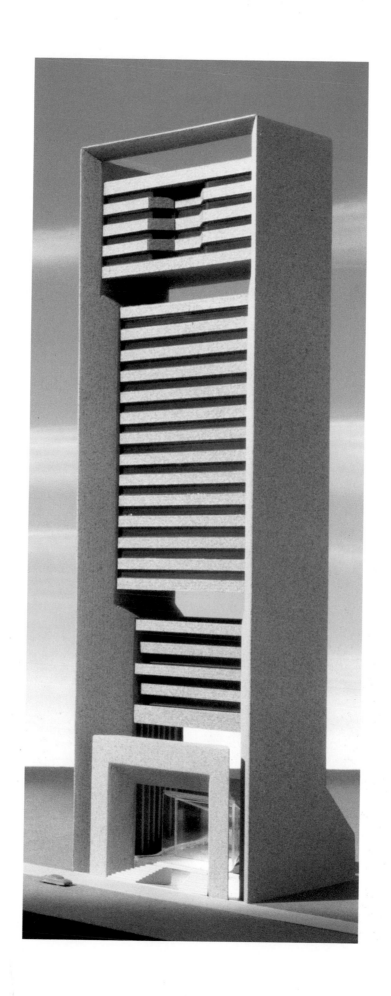

Casa De Retiro Espiritual
Cordoba, Spain

Located 45 miles from Cordoba, in the middle of a wide and rolling wheat field, the house is used as a weekend retreat by a couple.

The house is a contemporary reformulation of the traditional Andalusian house, centered around the patio, onto which all rooms open. To keep the house cool in the hot-dry climate of Southern Spain, the living area is insulated by earth.

Two tall, rough stuccoed, white walls meet at a right angle, creating an envelope for the house and defining its entrance. From this entrance, steps of increasingly greater length lead down to an open air patio on to which the house opens. An ambulatory defines the patio's other two sides, and serves as a transition between the house and the patio. The house consists, simply, of a large continuous space, contained by sinuous walls, with different areas defined by smooth cavities excavated into the floor and echoed by the ceiling above. Floor and perimeter walls are covered with delicately colored small glass tiles, washed by the soft, diffused light descending from the skylights and the breezy light entering from the small curvilinear patio counterpointing the orthogonal one.

The building technique, as practiced by local builders, is concrete and bricks: concrete floor and wall slabs rest on beds of cast sand; a liner of fiberglass, fused at the seams, is wrapped entirely around the buried surfaces. Insulated double walls and slender columns support a concrete roof vaulted in several places to help define living areas. An underground "canopy" of fiberglass panels extends horizontally as a ten foot cornice from the wall's top to keep water from soaking the ground around the house.

All practical needs and services (kitchen, baths, storage, etc.) are satisfied by geometric containers placed into the ground. Sleeping is in some of the living areas or in the sleeping alcoves contained within the sides.

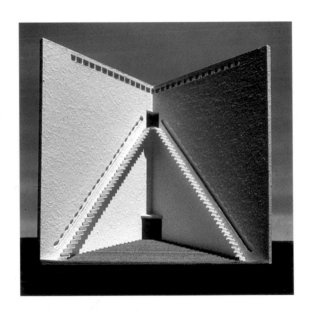

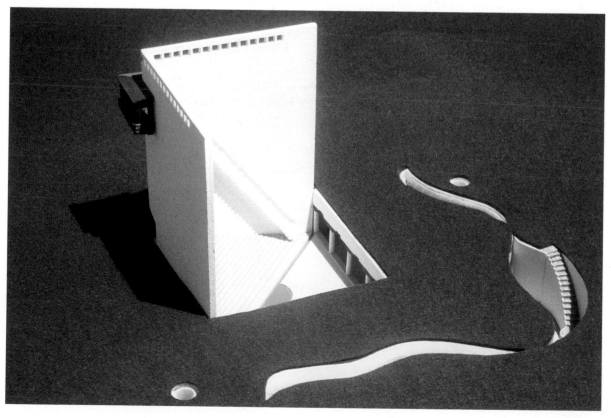

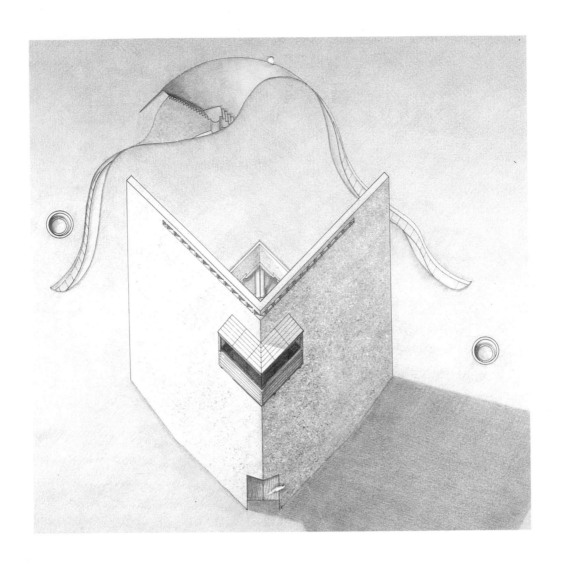

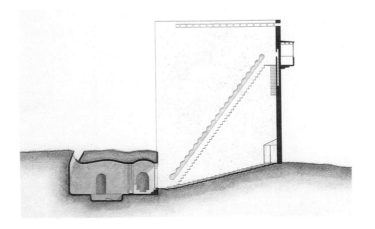

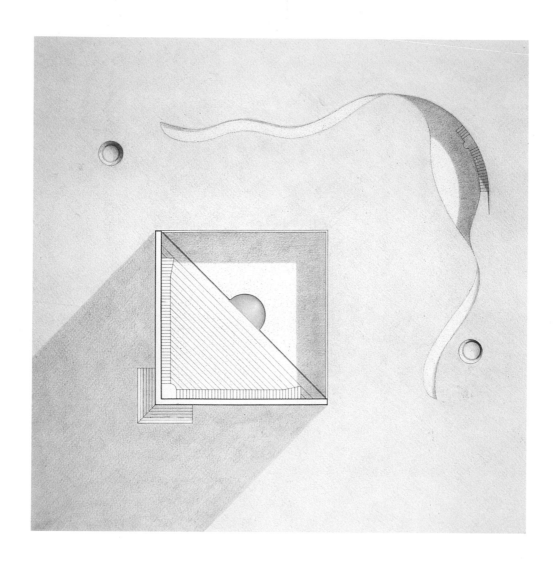

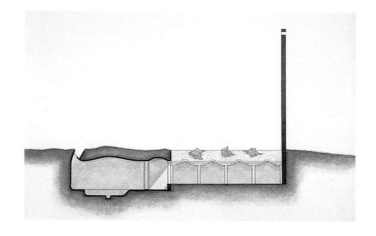

Pro Memoria Garden
Ludenhausen, West Germany

This project won a competition sponsored by the people of Ludenhausen, a small town south of Hannover. Completely rebuilt after World War II, Ludenhausen's physical recovery is so accomplished that none of the town's younger generations seem to remember its recent sad history. Determined that their children should not forget the grief and destruction that were brought about by war, the townspeople called for proposals that would serve as reminders of the evils of war and as object lessons in living together in peace.

This project, which draws on the Lower Saxony tradition of providing pensioners with a small plot of land on which to cultivate vegetables and flowers, proposes a large series of composite gardens. Each garden will consist of irregularly-shaped, one-fifth acre plots defined by seven foot high hedge walls and separated by narrow paths. Each plot is slightly different from the one next to it, and completely different from those far away. Children will be assigned, at birth, one of these plots, and when they are five years old, they will be taught the rudiments of gardening. It is hoped that, in this manner, they will learn about nature's laws and cycles, ultimately assuming responsibility for the plants and flowers entrusted to their care.

Whenever a plot is assigned, the newborn's name will be inscribed on a small marble slab that is placed within the plot's boundaries. When the plot's owner dies—ideally deep in years and heavy in wisdom—the marble slab will be turned upside down. The vacant garden will be reassigned to a newborn baby, and another marble slab, with the new gardener's name, will be placed next to the first one. The new gardener will be taught to respect the inheritance received, maintaining as well as improving it by introducing new ideas to enhance the planting.

The townspeople's implicit hope is that, in time, the gardeners will arrive at the idea of clipping away the hedges between the individual plots to create a large communal garden. At the same time, these people realize that some plots will remain the private joy of their individual owners, while others may be left to grow wild or barren through neglect. However, there may one day emerge communal gardens that still allow for the cultivation of individual plots.

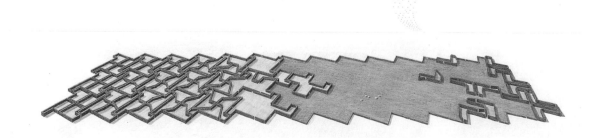

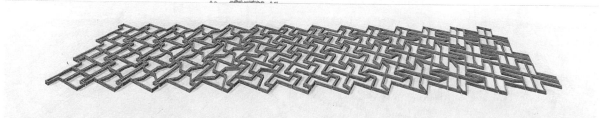

Banque Bruxelles Lambert
Lausanne, Switzerland

To many people, Lausanne evokes images of mountains, snow, lakes, steep streets, and quaint facades. However, this landscape of the mind rarely matches that of reality. The nearby peaks are often hidden by Lausanne's buildings, and there are few open spaces from which to contemplate the buildings themselves at a reasonable distance. Nevertheless, these images are pervasive ones, and are therefore recalled in the design of the bank's interior, in the hope that those entering it would, for an ineffable instant, discover that which they had always imagined but had, until then, seldom seen.

Upon entering the ground floor, the visitor finds himself in a serene, quietly luxurious atmosphere. Though actually quite small, the main hall, with ceilings barely nine feet high, seems lofty and capacious. The surrounding scene, which is deeply and ambiguously reflected in the midnight-blue lacquered ceiling, is that of far-away mountains, filtered through a soft, hazy light. Upon closer inspection, the haze reveals itself to be a curtain of fine silk yarn that hangs two meters in front of a trompe-l'oeil representation of mountains. On the left side of the main hall, a wall with three windows offers the approaching viewer a changing perspective of another mountain panorama, also rendered in the same sophisticated trompe-l'oeil technique. Inside has suddenly become Outside: the bank is transformed into an object in a landscape, sitting in an open, flat valley, surrounded by mountains. This inversion is then made literal, with bronze perspective strips converging along the floor on the facade of an architectural model of the bank building (the model conceals the doorway to the bank's safe directly behind).

Two Carrara marble counter tops, used for direct client transactions, are positioned to emphasize this illusion of vanishing perspective. Minimal in line, these objects assume an architectural role, as do the other pieces of furniture—pure volumes in black, white, and, as an occasional accent, red— contrapuntal elements in the landscape.

To integrate the ground and fifth floors and create a coherent whole, where light, space definition, and texture are unified, a special unit was developed for the fifth floor, similar to that used on the ground floor, which consists of a row of ceiling lights hidden by layers of hanging silk threads that diffuse light while creating a misty transparency. These curtains are used in all fifth-floor offices, as well as to define space in the main conference rooms, and to shield the windows of offices that face the street. Through these windows, the visitor sees the skyline of Lausanne. After having experienced the trompe-l'oeil landscape of the ground floor, he naturally expects this view to be yet another illusion, but he discovers, to his surprise, that he is looking at the *real* city. Thus, the cycle from illusion back to reality is complete.

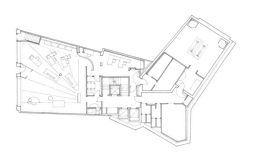

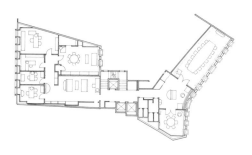

HOUSTON CENTER PLAZA
HOUSTON, TEXAS

The client for this project requested a plaza that would create a memorable image for the city of Houston. The site, one of the square blocks that is typical of the city's grid, will contain office buildings and a plaza with theaters, galleries, and restaurants, which will be connected to a convention center on an adjacent block. The design developed from a view of the plaza as a physical, metaphorical, and spiritual symbol of Houston.

The most outstanding feature of the city is precisely this grid; its strength being that it does not allow for a well-defined city center. Yet the very purity of the grid can be used as a foil to urban interventions. Thus, the grid of the city became the grid of the plaza, with a rough edge on the outside representing the incomplete nature of the growing city, and the square pool in the center representing the plaza itself.

The plaza is also meant to represent various aspects of Houston on a metaphorical level. The culture of the city is embodied in the theaters and galleries, the commerce in the shops, advanced technology in the laser exhibitions, and the life and energy of the city in the atrium that is at the heart of the shops and galleries. Most important of all, though, is the spiritual quality of the space. The outer part of the plaza consists of an array of trellises on a square grid covered by vines. The ground slopes down from the edge of the plaza to the large square pool in the center, with its circular opening above the atrium. The taller trellises toward the center serve as gazebos, with portals and seating. The plaza engages all the senses: colorful, fragrant flowers grow between the vines, and mist emanates from the top of each enclosure, thereby cooling the surroundings and producing a soothing hissing sound. The gazebos offer places for relaxation from office work and from the heat of the city, as well as places for socializing or quiet contemplation amid green shade.

The sense of cool retreat is reinforced by the water cascades around the square pool, and the circular waterfall inside the pool with its water continuing on as blades, splashing in the atrium space. The entire effect is reminiscent of Islamic Mogul gardens: the play of different sounds and textures of falling water; the lush vegetation; the cool shade. The garden is an appropriate one for Houston because it was designed for a climate that requires the refreshment of water and shade, and because its contemplative, spiritual environment offers an oasis in a growing city.

As an urban scale solution, the project recognizes its context on a local and city level. The plaza provides the visitor with a pleasant, memorable experience, and it also provides a unified, complex image that represents Houston on many levels.

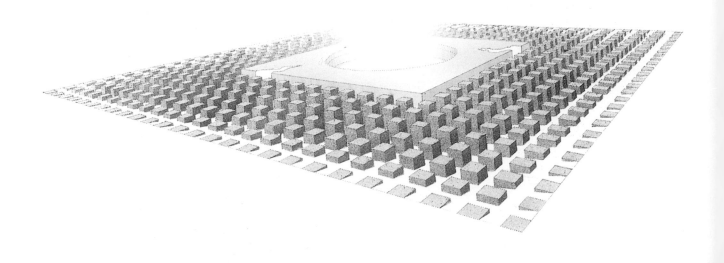

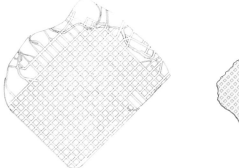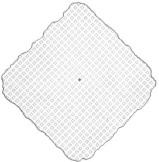

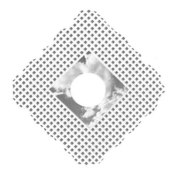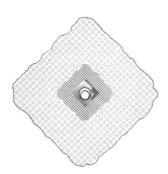

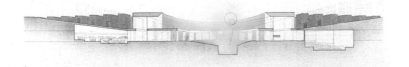

SCHLUMBERGER RESEARCH LABORATORIES
AUSTIN, TEXAS

The program for this computer research facility, to be built on a site outside Austin, required a laboratory that could adapt readily to changes in research-group size, and which would promote communication between individuals and groups. The solution offered a laboratory layout that met the client's programmatic needs while at the same time taking advantage of the building's site.

Because the site warranted a design that harmonized with the landscape rather than standing out against it, the project was divided into a series of smaller buildings with earth berms built up against them to help integrate them into the landscape, reduce energy costs, and provide the client the campus atmosphere requested. The buildings and recreational facilities are arranged casually around a man-made lake, in the manner of an English landscape garden. The buildings, because of the earth berms, blend into their surroundings, and provide a pleasant atmosphere for employees while taking advantage of the pleasant vistas. Furthermore, the separation of the buildings encourages workers to go out and experience the landscape, rather than simply observe it from an office window.

The laboratory design proposes a new type in the development of such spaces. It consists of a large, undifferentiated space in which the researchers' offices—9 × 9 foot mobile units—would be placed. The units, which contain desks and shelves, are totally enclosed, except for a door and window on opposite sides. The researcher has complete control over the lighting, acoustics, and temperature of his unit, and he also enjoys the privacy of a more traditional office. The mobile units may be moved quickly and easily by forklift to a new location to accommodate any group size and configuration. The proximity of these units and the common space that results from their arrangement fosters communication within the research group.

The laboratory design incorporates the best characteristics of the open office landscape—flexibility and ease of communication—with those of the traditional office, such as reduced noise levels, individual control of the environment, privacy, and a sense of permanence.

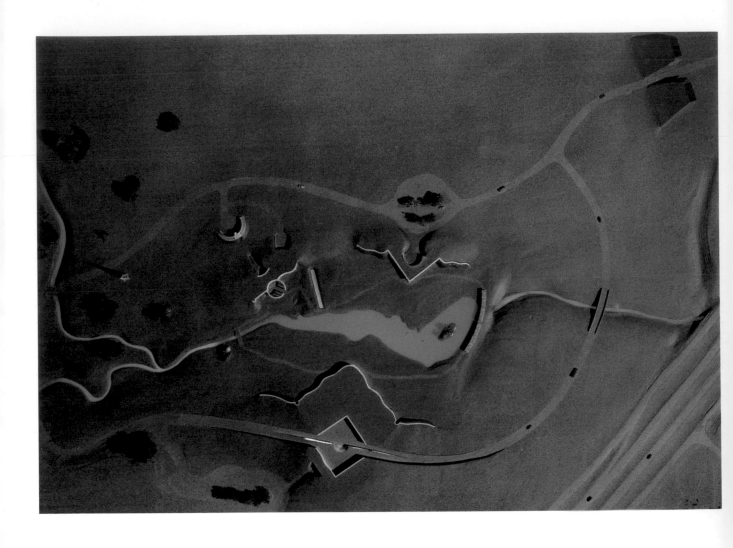

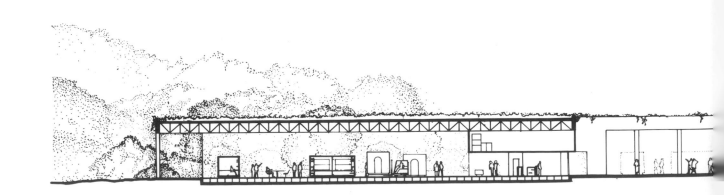

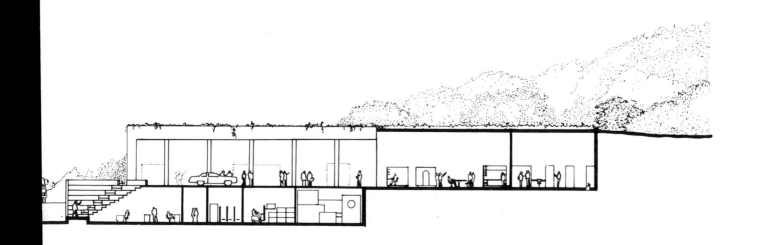

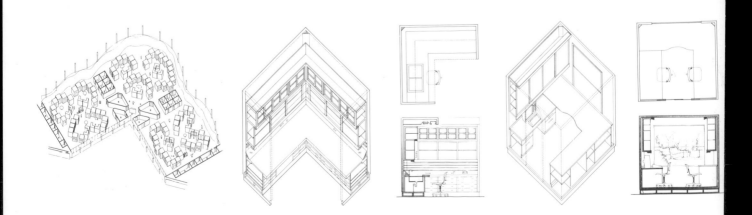

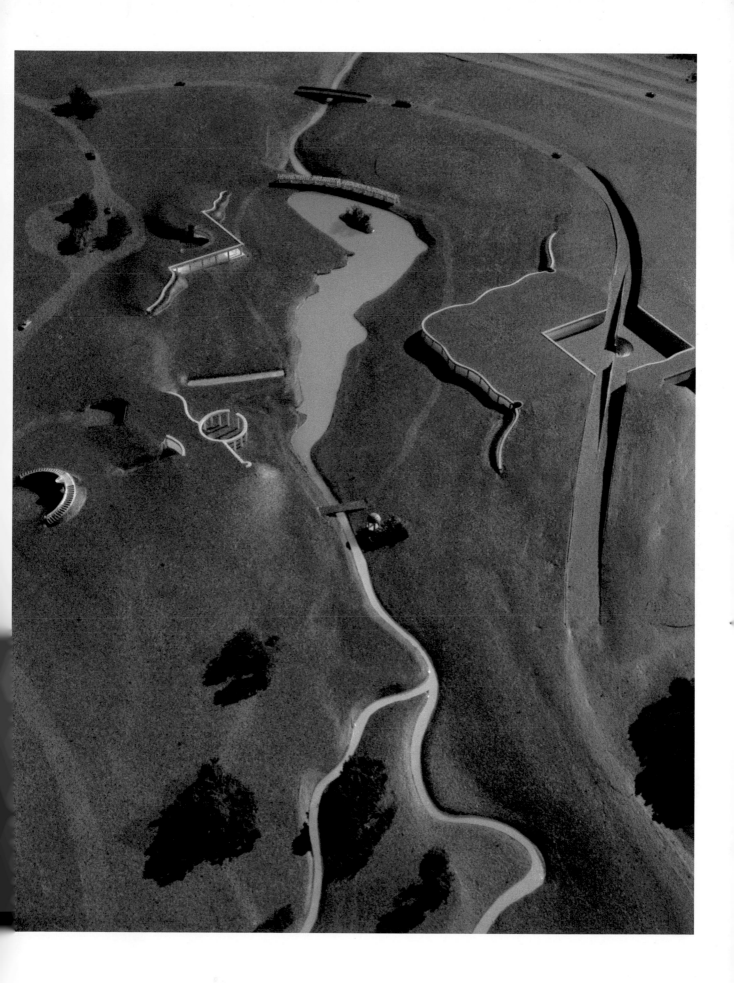

HOUSE FOR LEO CASTELLI
NORTHEAST, USA

Practical and wholesome, this house is at peace both with nature and the man-made environment. Two large earth berms serve as gates, shielding the house from the street and framing a grand entrance. They also provide an economical support for the solar panels that complement the passive solar design of the house. A gently terraced earth berm insulates the north-facing rooms and walls of the house, making it an integral, unobtrusive part of the landscape. Carefully planned cross-ventilation eliminates the need for air-conditioning. The combination of passive and active solar design slashes the house's heating requirements by 70% compared to those of a conventional design. Large windows face south to capture the sun's rays, and the thick walls of the house absorb and store heat.

The house contains a large living room and dining area, studio/library, master bedroom, three smaller bedrooms, guest room, four baths, large custom kitchen, laundry room, wine cellar, and ample storage space. The living area, located between the parents' and children's quarters, offers privacy to both. The open layout of the rooms allows a flexible organization of the interior spaces. All rooms open onto an arcaded courtyard, which also functions as a graceful entrance court.

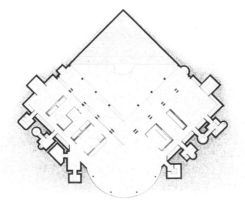
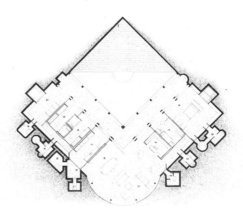

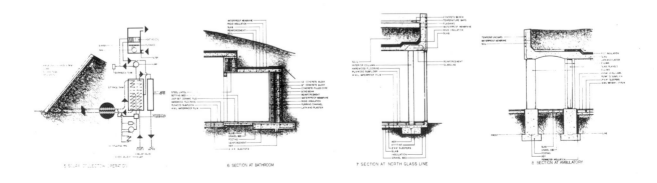

5 SOLAR COLLECTOR OPERATION   6 SECTION AT BATHROOM   7 SECTION AT NORTH GLASS LINE   8 SECTION AT AMBULATORY

PLAZA MAYOR
SALAMANCA, SPAIN

Salamanca, located in the middle of the Iberian peninsula, is one of the oldest cities in Europe. Since 300 BC, Celts, Romans, and Moors have conquered, destroyed, and reconstructed the city. Its university, one of the oldest and most prestigious in the world, ranks with those of Bologna, Paris, and London. The Tormes River nourishes a perennial greenbelt around the city, making it a magnet for civilization and distinguishing it from the region's dry surroundings.

Salamanca's Plaza Mayor is, in true Iberian fashion, the center of the city's commercial and cultural activity as well as a place of repose: it is to the city, what the city is to the surrounding province. Square and open, the Plaza stands in contrast to the dense and irregular pattern of the area's buildings and streets. Around the plaza is a four-sided baroque facade, designed by Churriguera, which is one of the glories of Spanish architecture. The columns of the ground-floor arcade separate commercial and private interests from the public plaza. The plaza itself is a flat, barren place, unsuited to sitting or gathering in either cold or hot weather, for which this design is intended to create a sheltered, tree-shaded space.

Concentric squares will step down towards the center of the plaza. Its floor is a circular patterned metal grating that lights a dance hall directly below it. The plaza's former ground level will be maintained by the tops of the trees, which create a metaphorical ground cover of leafy clouds. As one descends into the plaza, the tree trunks begin to emerge. These columnar trunks and the green canopy overhead allude to the arcaded loggia beneath the surrounding facades. Below this forested plaza are cinemas, theaters, gymnasiums, community offices and, in keeping with one of the plaza's traditional uses, the dance hall. An air pocket between the steps and these public functions acts as a plenum, trapping shaded air to cool the plaza in summer. In winter, when the leaves have fallen, the sun strikes the exposed plaza, warming its stone steps.

The new Plaza Mayor grows physically as well as symbolically from the very stone of the city, offering both a quiet, shaded retreat, and a hub of public activity.

BANQUE BRUXELLES LAMBERT
NEW YORK CITY, NEW YORK

The New York branch of the Banque Bruxelles Lambert, Belgium, houses 20,000 square feet of executive and operational offices, a trading room, computer rooms, conference rooms, a board room, and support areas, and gives architectural form to the client's wish to become an accepted part of its host city.

The words "New York" and "Manhattan" invariably evoke images of tall buildings, but this imaginary cityscape seldom matches what we see in reality. Tall buildings hide other tall buildings, and there is rarely enough open space to afford a comfortable perspective of their facades. Still their presence is pervasive. This design provides that perspective within the bank's offices by "opening its windows" and making the walls "transparent." It admits illusionistic views of the city outside and, in the process, creates the impression of greater spaciousness than actually exists.

The reception area establishes a serene and luxurious atmosphere. This small and typically low-ceilinged space is made to seem far more spacious than it really is by means of a trompe-l'oeil depiction of city views, seen as if they were nearby. A suspended ceiling is made of two layers of fabric placed four inches apart, which create a lacy moire pattern, and veil the "star" lights that are placed at different heights in the black night of ducts and electrical conduits. The illusion of depth is heightened by filtering the photographs of the tall buildings through a curtain of fine silk threads that mimic the effect of smoggy city air. In the operational area, the walls are pierced by "windows" that offer other panoramic views. The freestanding partitions that define private work areas assume the role of buildings in a cityscape, an illusion that is heightened by a grid-patterned carpet that emphasizes perspective. And the simple, minimal volumes of the highly-polished, lacquered black desks and cabinets reflect the surrounding "city views." Each object, although starkly plain in line, takes on added dimensions.

In the executive offices, the illusionistic game is revealed: the views beyond the curtained windows are those of the real Manhattan skyline, surprising the visitor who expects yet another trompe-l'oeil panorama.

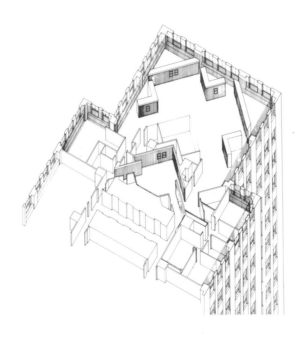

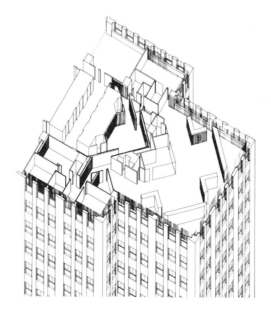

Elective Affinities
Milan, Italy

Twenty-one internationally known architects were invited to participate in the exhibition "Elective Affinities" for the Milan Triennale in 1983. The exhibition's title, which refers to a Goethe text of the same name, provided a thematic framework. Each designer was given a platform surrounded by ramped walls and supported on one side by two wooden columns. Underneath the platform and inaccessible from the ramped walls, but visually open on the sides and front, are placed elements antecedent to design, strong forces of memory.

On the platform itself, a modular shelving system assumes the form of a room or "studiolo" where nature is reconciled with culture: books on the inside share a common wall with plants on the outside. In the "grotto," symbolically located in the base of the platform, both realms come together. This reconciliation of the cultured and the cultivated represents the precarious moment when the fragile man-made edifice sits upon the crust of a seething magma of volcanic forces and violent natural undercurrents.

Earth, air, water, and fire clash violently and are perceived only dimly through the circular grate in the platform floor. The sound that emanates anticipates the end of all matter.

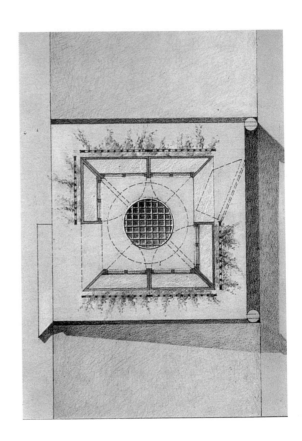

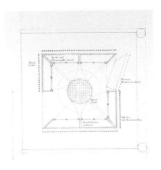

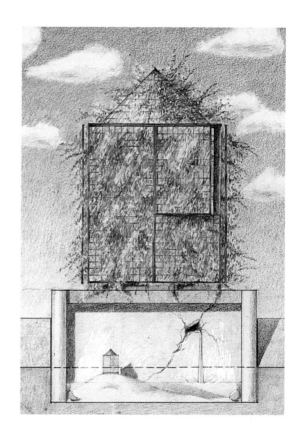

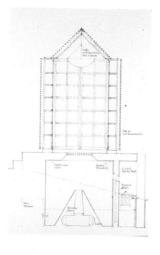

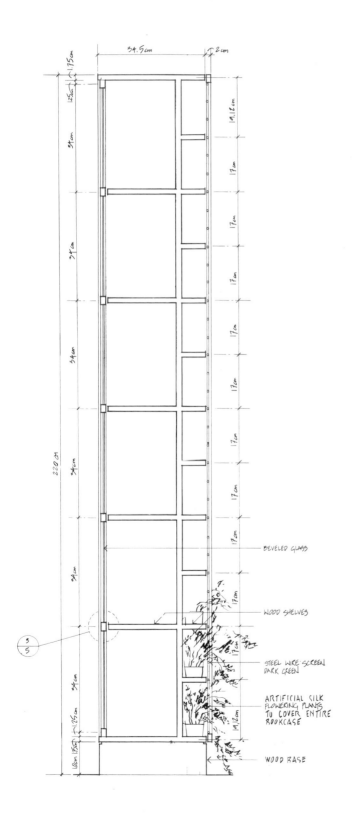

34.5cm

2cm

220 cm

BEVELED GLASS

WOOD SHELVES

STEEL WIRE SCREEN
DARK GREEN

ARTIFICIAL SILK
FLOWERING PLANTS
TO COVER ENTIRE
BOOKCASE

WOOD BASE

3/5

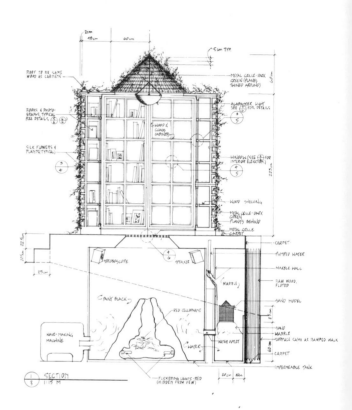

ROOF TO BE SAME
WOOD AS CABINETS

BOOKS & PHOTO-
GRAPHS TYPICAL
SEE DETAILS

SILK FLOWERS &
PLANTS TYPICAL

5cm TYP.

METAL GRILLE · DARK
GREEN (PLANTS)
SHINED AROUND)

ALABASTER LIGHT
SEE ③ FOR DETAILS

WOOD &
GLASS
CABINETS

WINDOW (SEE ④ FOR
INTERIOR ELEVATION)

WOOD SHELVING

METAL GRILLE · DARK
GREEN
PLANTS BEHIND

METAL GRILLE ·
CARPET

STROBOSCOPE

SPEAKER

CARPET

PUMPED WATER

MARBLE WALL

MARBLE

RAW WOOD,
FLUTED

PAINT BLACK

RED CELLOPHANE

SAND MODEL

SAND

MARBLE

SURFACE SAME AS RAMPED WALK

WAVE-MAKING
MACHINE

WATER

WATER OUTLET

CARPET

IMPERMEABLE TANK

FLICKERING LIGHTS · RED
(HIDDEN FROM VIEW)

①/③ SECTION 1:15 M

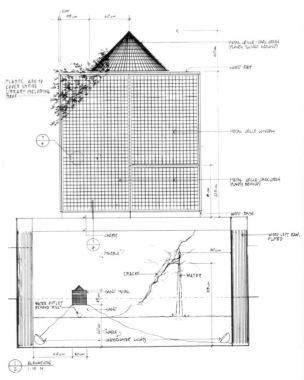

PLANTS ARE TO
COVER ENTIRE
LIBRARY INCLUDING
ROOF

METAL GRILLE · DARK GREEN
(PLANTS SHINED AROUND)

WOOD ROOF

METAL GRILLE WINDOW

METAL GRILLE · DARK
GREEN (PLANTS BEHIND)

WOOD BASE

WOOD LEFT RAW,
FLUTED

CARPET

MARBLE

CRACKS

WATER

SAND MODEL

WATER OUTLET
BEYOND "HILL"

SAND

WATER ·
UNDERWATER LIGHTS

①/② ELEVATION 1:15 M

NEW ORLEANS MUSEUM OF ART,
NEW ORLEANS, LOUISIANA

This project was one of six finalists, chosen from among 750 submissions, in a national competition for the design of an expansion for the New Orleans Museum of Art. The museum, housed in a classical building, itself the product of an earlier competition, is located on a site that is essentially flat, except for a slight slope down to the edge of a lagoon. The lagoon is part of an interconnecting, man-made system for recreational boating and fishing that meanders through the City Park.

Rather than attempting to add to the existing building and altering its classical bearing, this design takes advantage of the lagoons by creating a series of floating galleries, which can be rearranged to suit the demands of changing exhibitions.

Two automated boats will carry visitors and make deliveries to the archipelago of exhibition spaces, to the floating restaurant, and to the museum shop. The logistical requirements of shipping, receiving, and storage are resolved by building new spaces on land, adjacent to the old museum, thereby eliminating the need to change established patterns of traffic and delivery. In these new spaces, administrative offices and reference areas will enjoy views of the lagoon while maintaining a direct physical connection to the old building. The roof of the administrative offices will provide a grand esplanade to enhance the ceremonial approach and entrance to the new galleries. The long, boulevard-like approach to the old museum, actually a turf covered underground parking garage, preserves the sylvan nature of the museum's park setting.

In this project, water is the great conciliator. The classical facade of the old building, which fancies itself eternal, is wedded nautically to the more pragmatic floating containers, which know themselves to be temporary. This betrothal is celebrated by the half ring of the pier, which completes itself only in its reflection in the water. This high-tech structure becomes the gate between the old museum and the new.

East Elevation

South Elevation

East Section

East Section

South Section

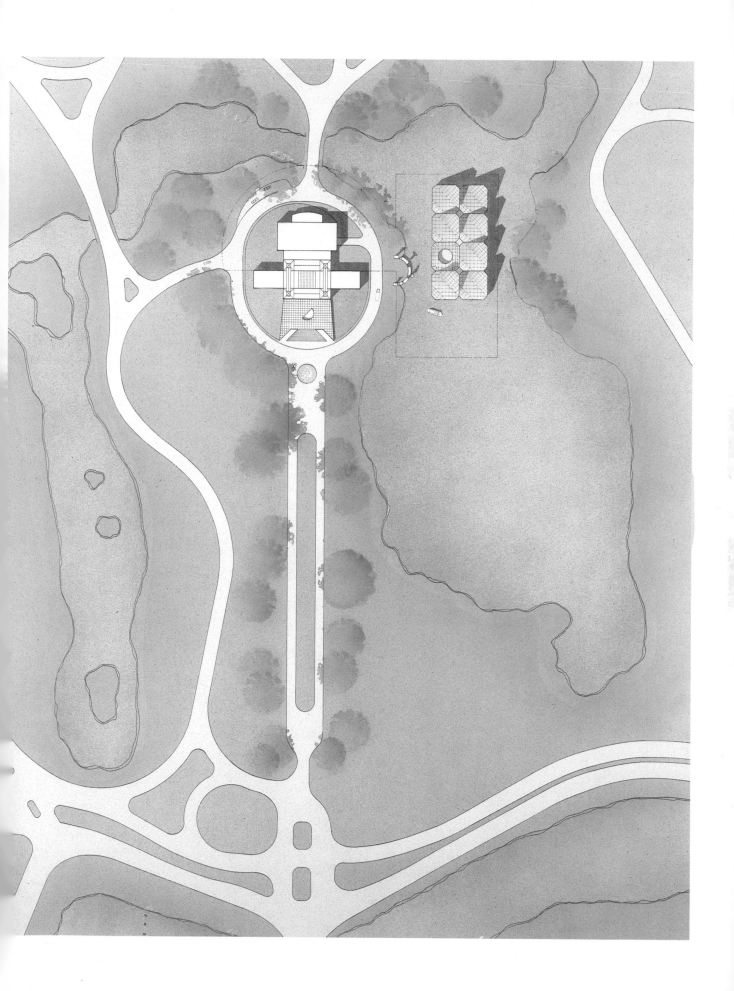

Emilio's Folly: Man is an Island

No, I never thought about it in words. It came to me as a full-fledged, irreducible image, like a vision.

I fancied myself the owner of a wide grazing field, somewhere in the fertile plains of Texas or the province of Buenos Aires. In the middle of this field was a partly sunken, open-air construction. I felt as if this place had always existed. Its entrance was marked by a baldachine, held up by three columns, which in turn supported a lemon tree. From the entrance, a triangular earthen plane stepped gently toward the diagonal of a large, sunken square courtyard which was half earth, half water. From the center of the courtyard rose a rocky mass that resembled a mountain. On the water floated a barge made of logs, sheltered by a thatched roof and supported by wooden trusses that rested on four square-sectioned wooden pillars. With the aid of a long pole the barge could be sculled into an opening in the mountain. Once inside this cave, one could land the barge on cove-like shore illuminated by a zenithal opening. More often, I used the barge to reach an L-shaped cloister where I could read, draw, or just think, sheltered from the wind and sun. The cloister was defined on the outside by a water basin, and on the inside by a number of undulating planes that screened alcove-like spaces. Once I discovered their entrances, I began to use them for storage.

Although I am not compulsively driven to order and thrive, instead, on tenuously controlled disorder, I decided to use these alcoves in an orderly sequence, storing things in the first alcove until it was full, and then proceeding clockwise to the next one. The first items I stored were my childhood toys, school notebooks, stamp collection and a few items of clothing to which I had become attached. Later, I started moving out of the house and into the second alcove gifts I had received while doing my military service, as well as my uniform. I became fond of traversing the water basin once in a while to dress up in it, to make sure that I had not put on too much weight.

Not all the things I stored in these alcoves were there because they had given me pleasure, but I could not rid myself of them. In time, I developed a technique for using these things to support other objects. I often wondered whether I was going to run out of space, but somehow always found extra room, either by reorganizing things or because some objects had shrunk or collapsed because of their age or from the weight of the items that had accumulated on top of them.

On the diagonal axis passing the entrance canopy, but directly above it, an undulating plane was missing. Instead of a storage alcove, there was an entrance to a man-height tunnel that lead to an open pit filled with a fresh mist. I never understood where this cold-water mist originated, but it never failed to produce a rainbow.

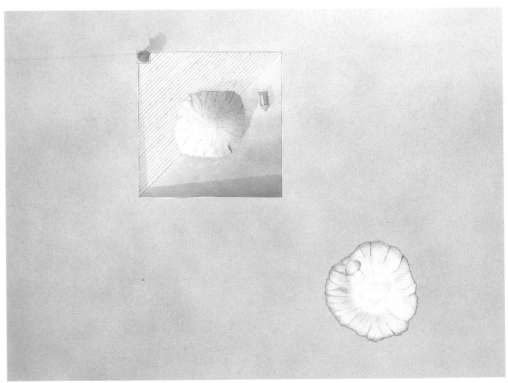

ESCHENHEIMER TOWER
FRANKFURT, WEST GERMANY

The City of Frankfurt sponsored an invited competition for the design of a pedestrian street connecting the Eschenheimer Tower, formerly the gate to the city, to a pedestrian area 1,000 feet away; the new walkway was to utilize the existing Schillerstrasse. This design, which won first place, not only met the competition's stated requirements, but went beyond them to propose an urbanistic solution to a severe, chronic traffic problem at the Tower.

The Eschenheimer Tower stands on the site of the old city walls, which were removed in the 19th Century to make room for a ring road around Frankfurt. This 700 foot wide, heavily-traveled ring road is considered by pedestrians to be too hazardous to cross and the underground passages beneath the road too squalid. In desperation, some pedestrians resort to taking the tram to cross the road.

Because the city's traffic department would not allow any traffic lanes to be moved or even disrupted, nor would it allow any traffic signals to be displaced, this design proposes the creation of a barrel vault to enclose the ring road. The vault would be covered with earth to create a gently rolling hill which would provide a "bridge" for pedestrians. This hill would become a landscaped mini-park uniting inner and outer sectors of the city, until now separated by the ring road. This bridge concept could easily be duplicated at other points along the ring road, taking advantage of the many interrupted landscaped areas that exist along the ring road. By covering these cross roads with the same landscaped bridges, those patches of greenery would be connected, transforming the ring road into a greenbelt around the city, to be enjoyed by pedestrians, joggers, bicycle riders, and drivers. In this way, the Eschenheimer Tower becomes a gateway, serving as a garden foyer for the entire city, while defining the edge of the urban fabric.

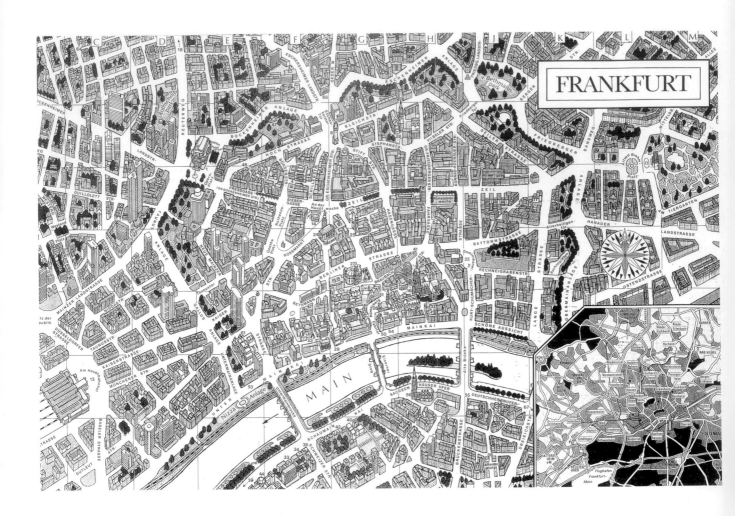

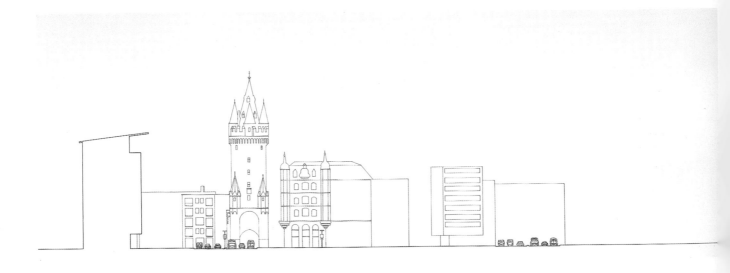

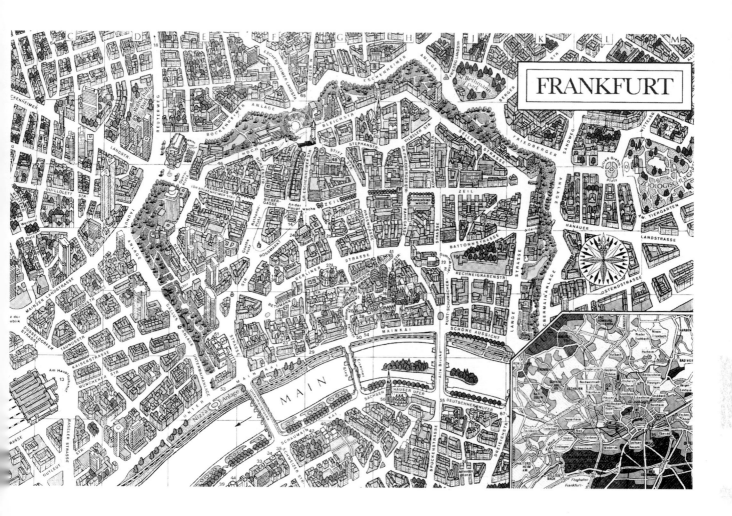

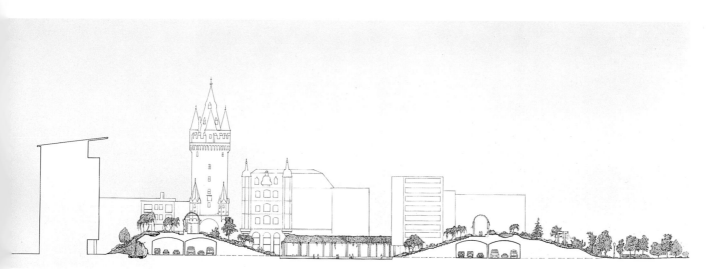

Ansicht der Arkade

Querschnitt

Grundriß

FINANCIAL GUARANTY INSURANCE COMPANY
NEW YORK CITY, NEW YORK

The Financial Guaranty Insurance Company (FGIC) is a rapidly growing firm that sells insurance for municipal bonds. Since FGIC does not sell a tangible product, the impression made by its offices became highly important. The various elements of the design are orchestrated into an unfolding series of "landscape" vignettes. Curtains of gauzy silk strings that transmit light like fiber optics are used as partitions, screening views while hinting at a presence beyond. Each executive office and conference room is ringed with these curtains of light. Shimmering behind them, a blue wall covering, gradually intensifying in tone from bottom to top, gives the illusion of a far horizon. Standing in the center of the room, a visitor feels surrounded by windows in an aerie high above the city.

The materials are layered with patterns and textures that act as veils, giving them greater depth and modulating them in space. The painted walls are not a single color but, like an eggshell, are spattered with many shades of grey and lilac. The ceilings are gridded with a pattern of disks, actually sprinklerhead covers that create a Cartesian plane of "coordinates" with their slightly reflective surfaces. The carpet mirrors this pattern in lines of hand-cut circles that lead the eye toward an ever-changing vanishing point. This geometry is also repeated in the glass of the partitions and windows, which is patterned with a grid of clear hemispheres that emphasizes the ephemeral quality of the transparent material.

Mobility is the second theme of the design. The flexibility needed for teamwork is accommodated by an open-office environment into which self-contained, modular work units are inserted. These offices are based on a type first developed for the Schlumberger Research Laboratories. Like a box within a box, each six-by-eight foot unit can be picked up with a fork lift and moved like furniture. The ceilings, constructed of fabric panels over acoustical louvers, are porous enough to permit air flow while ensuring auditory privacy. Glass walls admit abundant natural light and allow visual contact between workers, fostering a sense of community. The occupant of each unit controls task lighting and ventilation. By clustering the units in different ways, various work organizations can be accommodated. The corridor between the units becomes communal space, rather than merely circulation, and the mobility of the units allows flexibility in meeting the demand of work flow, group activities, and the expansion or contraction of group size.

As a visitor moves through the office, the experience is one of a series of separate visual episodes. But, as in an English garden, glimpses of the next vignette hint at what is around the corner. While the context is that of a sleek, modern office space with a full complement of modern equipment and conveniences, the visitor leaves with the impression of quietly functional elegance, of spaces only partially seen and understood, but which add to a smoothly run, finely wrought totality.

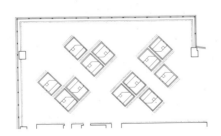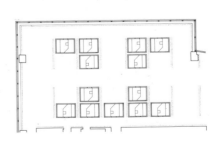

MERCEDES BENZ SHOWROOM
NEW JERSEY

The program for this project specified the design of a showroom for new Mercedes Benz automobiles. The site is quite small with a tree covered hill in the background but with typical commercial buildings to its left. In order to hide these buildings from the view of the people approaching the showroom via the primary road access, a tall wall of polished black stone will be erected. This reflective black wall will serve as a display board as well as backdrop against which to profile the new vehicles.

Since a showroom concerned with the display of cars should evoke a feeling of movement, the exhibition spaces, both exterior and interior, have been conceived as a continuous ramped surface that leads both up and down from the road level. The enclosed showroom consists of translucent glass block floors that are inclined in such a way that visitors to the showroom are always provided a sense of movement and are able to view cars from above and below as well as laterally.

The cars, presented as sculpture, suggest acceleration and deceleration; and the translucent glass plane, dematerialized by the light passing through it, further emphasizes the poetic aspect of movement.

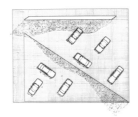

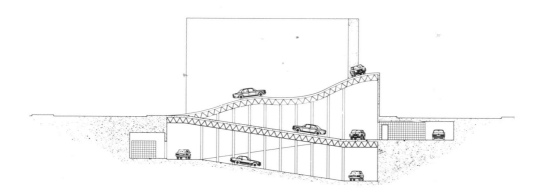

189.

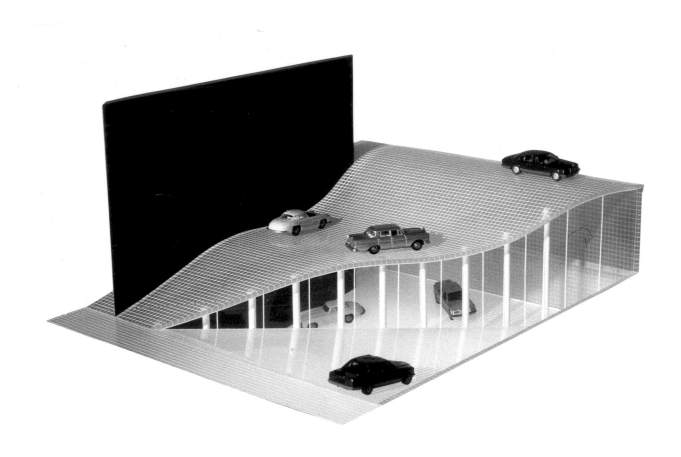

RESIDENCE-AU-LAC
LUGANO, SWITZERLAND

The Residence-au-Lac, which overlooks Lake Lugano, was built in the 1950s as a resort hotel. Its present owner, who converted the building into luxury apartments, sought to enliven its 46 foot wide, 100 foot long terrace, which is visible from the lakefront avenue and gardens and commands a panoramic view of the mountains surrounding Lugano. This view of mountains, sky, and clouds is recreated on the terrace and in the building's lobby.

The terrace continues into the building and ultimately becomes the lobby floor. It is made of four inch wide slabs of rough-finished granite alternating with four/fifths inch wide strips of polished white Carrara marble. These marble strips emerge at irregular intervals, forming jagged shapes that echo the mountains on the horizon. Inside the lobby, where the walls are painted a gradient blue to suggest the distant sky, the mountainous marble landscape takes on an even more surrealistic air under translucent silk "clouds" hanging from a top-lit blue plexiglass ceiling. The clouds are spaced at regular intervals, corresponding to the spacing of the jagged marble forms, to echo the effect of the clouds that pass over the real mountains outside. In this way architecture, sculpture, and landscape merge into a dreamlike whole.

MASTER PLAN FOR THE UNIVERSAL EXPOSITION—SEVILLE, 1992
SEVILLE, SPAIN

Twelve architects from around the world were invited to participate in a competition to design a master plan for the Universal Exposition to celebrate the 500th anniversary of the discovery of America, to be held in Seville in 1992. This proposal won the First Prize and the Gold Medal.

The history of world expositions demonstrates that few were designed with the future in mind. Most of them left behind frightening ruins, in the form of roads, buildings, bridges, monorails, cable cars, etc., that had to be abandoned because they had no useful purpose beyond the span of the exposition. The most notable exception to this rule is that of the World Exhibition of 1892 in Chicago, which left as its magnificent legacy Jackson Park. It stands as a glorious tribute not only to its designer, Frederick Law Olmstead, but to the farsightedness of the exhibition's organizers.

Without a clear image of the future, it is impossible to effect significant changes in the present. Therefore, in order to design for 1992, it is essential to design for 1993. With this in mind, and given the fact that the magnificent city of Seville has no grand suburban green space in the style of Jackson Park, it seemed appropriate to create a park that would belong to the city long after the exposition was gone. The park's design would have to satisfy the urban needs of the city as well as the complex requirements of a world exposition. Water and shade were deemed to be the elements that could best satisfy both sets of needs in a unique manner.

Water is, historically, the great communications link between Spain and the New World. The site of the exposition is 531 acres of the island of Cartuja in the Gualalquivir River. Given the premise that what is left behind in 1993 is just as important as what is designed for 1992, it is essential to develop an image of the future in order to guide the architects of the present.

The master plan proposes three large lagoons on which most of the activity of the exposition takes place, and which will later become the core of this magnificent park. Ferry boats move visitors (22 million are expected) around the exposition efficiently and pleasantly, eliminating the need for costly roads and transportation systems that would be of little use after the exposition. For the 60 nations and the many corporations and organizations that are expected to participate, temporary pavilions on barges offer an economical alternative to the expense of constructing in-ground foundations and the last-minute rush to build extra roads and facilities.

The second key element in the exposition design, given the warm climate of Seville, is that of shade. Earth removed from the lagoons creates three hills, covered with greenery, which provide not only shade but a backdrop for the exposition and for the theaters, auditoriums, and sports stadium that will be the exposition's

only permanent buildings. The exposition and its parking areas are cooled by numerous shade trees, and by cold water mist from nozzles located on arbors 35 feet above the ground. These cooling measures should reduce the temperature in the exposition area seven to ten degrees (Fahrenheit) below that of the city.

The master plan also looks well beyond 1993, the year that the exposition grounds become a park for Seville. Some of its permanent elements will be used as an administrative center for the University of Seville. All the building for the university, colleges as well as dormitories, would again be located on floating pavilions in the third lagoon, near the sporting facilities that will remain a permanent fixture of the park. The university project should be completed by the year 2003.

A drastic departure from traditional world's fair design, this master plan is consistent with the Grand Theme of the 1992 Universal Exposition—"The Era of Discovery"—and its emphasis on invention and innovation throughout history and in the future.

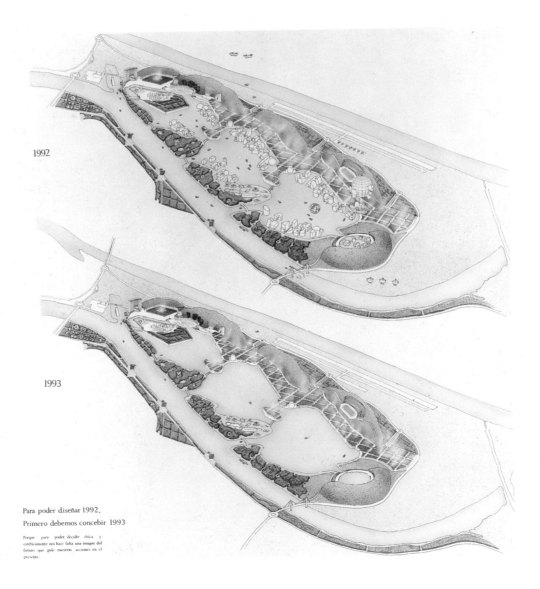

1992

1993

Para poder diseñar 1992,
Primero debemos concebir 1993

Porque para poder decidir ética y
estéticamente nos hace falta una imagen del
futuro que guíe nuestras acciones en el
presente.

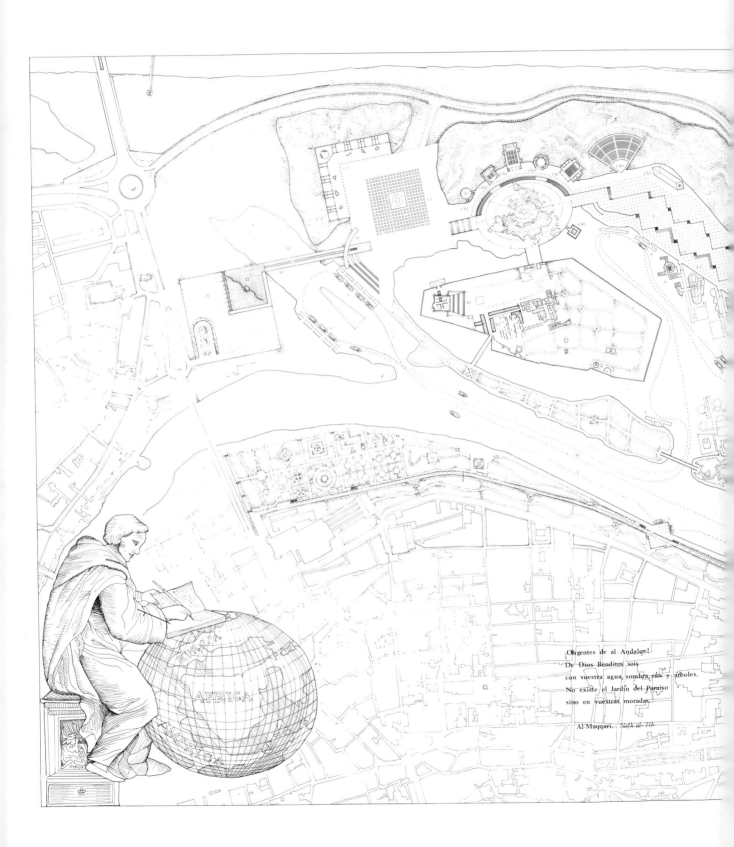

¡Orientes de al-Andalus!
De Dios Benditos sois
con vuestra agua, sombra, ríos y árboles.
No existe el Jardín del Paraíso
sino en vuestras moradas.

Al-Maqqari, *Nafh al-Tib*

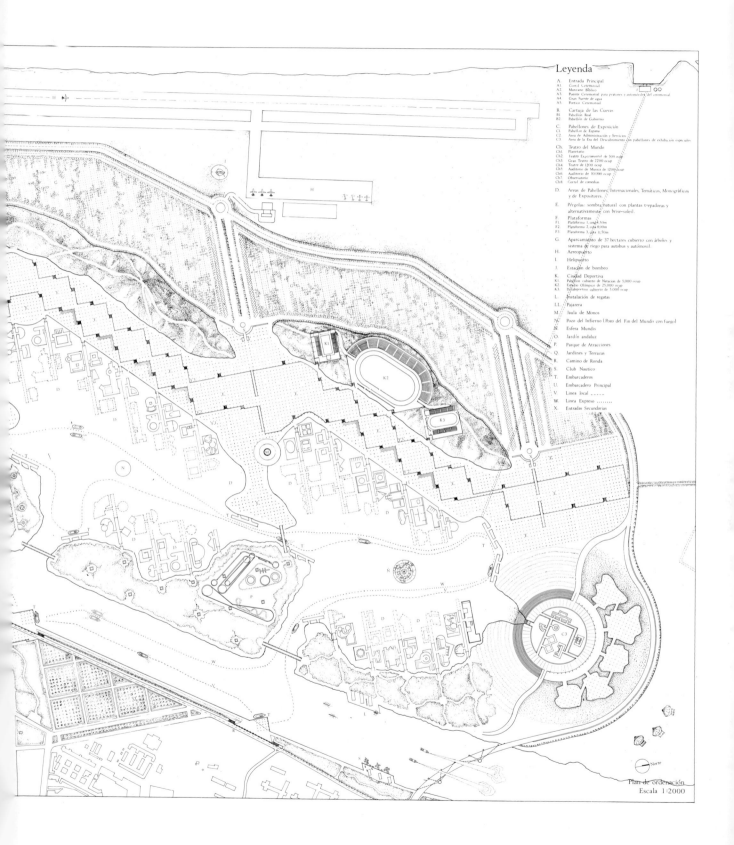

Leyenda

A. Entrada Principal
A.1 Corril Ceremonial
A.2 Manzano Bíblico
A.3 Puente Ceremonial para peatones y automóviles del ceremonial
A.4 Gran Fuente de agua
A.5 Pórtico Ceremonial

B. Cartuja de las Cuevas
B.1 Pabellón Real
B.2 Pabellón de Gobierno

C. Pabellones de Exposición
C.1 Pabellón de España
C.2 Área de Administración y Servicios
C.3 Área de la Era del Descubrimiento con pabellones de exhibición especiales

Ch. Teatro del Mundo
Ch.1 Planetario
Ch.2 Teatro Experimental de 500 ocup
Ch.3 Gran Teatro de 2200 ocup
Ch.4 Teatro de 1200 ocup
Ch.5 Auditorio de Música de 1200 ocup
Ch.6 Auditorio de 10.000 ocup
Ch.7 Observatorio
Ch.8 Corral de comedias

D. Áreas de Pabellones Internacionales, Temáticos, Monográficos y de Expositores.

E. Pérgolas: sombra natural con plantas trepadoras y alternativamente con brise-soleil.

F. Plataformas
F.1 Plataforma 1, cota 9,50m
F.2 Plataforma 2, cota 8,00m
F.3 Plataforma 3, cota 11,50m

G. Aparcamiento de 37 hectáreas cubierto con árboles y sistema de riego para autobús y automóvil.

H. Aeropuerto

I. Helipuerto

J. Estación de bombeo

K. Ciudad Deportiva
K.1 Pabellón cubierto de Natación de 5.000 ocup
K.2 Estadio Olímpico de 25.000 ocup
K.3 Polideportivo cubierto de 5.000 ocup

L. Instalación de regatas

LL. Pajarera

M. Jaula de Monos

N. Pozo del Infierno (Pozo del Fin del Mundo con fuego)

Ñ. Esfera Mundis

O. Jardín andaluz

P. Parque de Atracciones

Q. Jardines y Terrazas

R. Camino de Ronda

S. Club Náutico

T. Embarcaderos

U. Embarcadero Principal

V. Línea local _ _ _ _ _

W. Línea Expreso . . . .

X. Entradas Secundarias

Norte

Plan de ordenación
Escala 1:2000

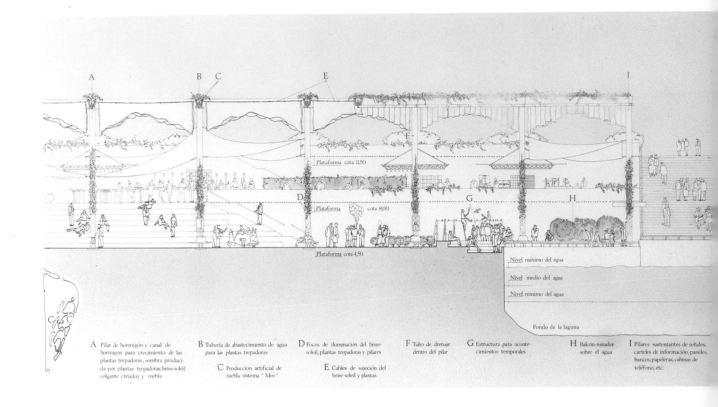

Plataforma cota 11.50

Plataforma   cota 8.00

Plataforma cota 4,50

Nivel máximo del agua

Nivel medio del agua

Nivel mínimo del agua

Fondo de la laguna

A Pilar de hormigón y canal de
hormigón para crecimiento de las
plantas trepadoras; sombra producida por plantas trepadoras, brise-soleil
colgante (tejido) y niebla

B Tubería de abastecimiento de agua
para las plantas trepadoras

C Producción artificial de
niebla sistema "Mec"

D Focos de iluminación del brise-
soleil, plantas trepadoras y pilares

E Cables de sujeción del
brise-soleil y plantas

F Tubo de drenaje
dentro del pilar

G Estructura para aconte-
cimientos temporales

H Balcón-mirador
sobre el agua

I Pilares sustentantes de señales,
carteles de información, paneles,
bancos, papeleras, cabinas de
teléfono, etc.

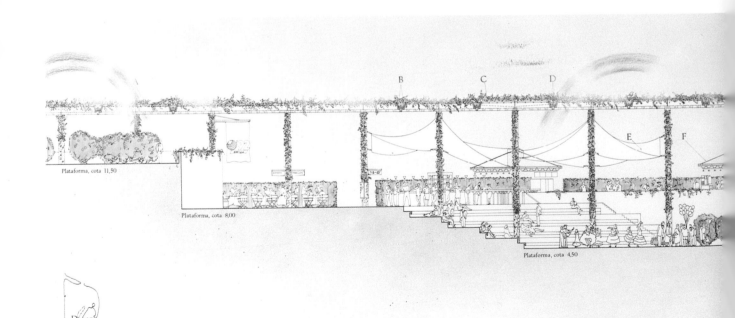

Plataforma, cota 11,50

Plataforma, cota 8,00

Plataforma, cota 4,50

A Pilar de hormigón y canal de
hormigón para crecimiento de las
plantas trepadoras - sombra producida
por plantas trepadoras, brise-soleil
colgante (tejidos) y niebla.

B Producción artificial de
niebla, sistema "Mec".

C Cables de sujeción del brise-soleil
y plantas trepadoras.

D Tubo de drenaje
dentro del pilar.

E Carpas Temporales,(tejido brise-

F Carpas te
metálica y

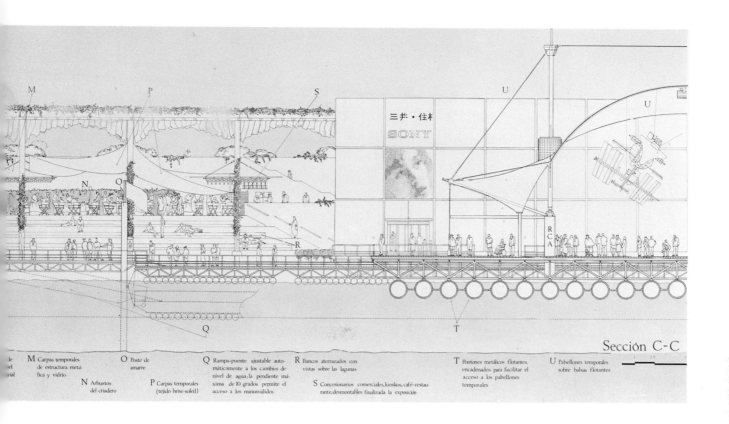

三井・住友
SONY

RCA

Sección C-C

M Carpas temporales
   de estructura metá-
   lica y vidrio

N Arbustos
   del criadero

O Poste de
   amarre

P Carpas temporales
   (tejido brise-soleil)

Q Rampa-puente ajustable automáticamente a los cambios de
   nivel de agua, la pendiente máxima de 10 grados permite el
   acceso a los minusválidos

R Bancos aterrazados con
   vistas sobre las lagunas

S Concesionarios comerciales, kioskos, café-restau-
   rante, desmontables finalizada la exposición

T Pontones metálicos flotantes,
   encadenados para facilitar el
   acceso a los pabellones
   temporales

U Pabellones temporales
   sobre balsas flotantes

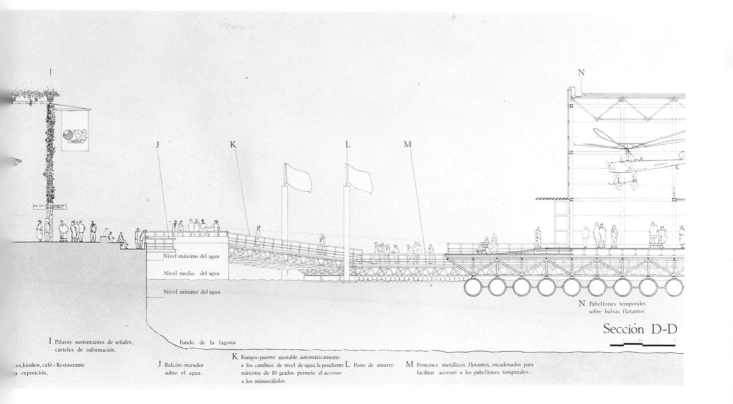

92

Nivel máximo del agua

Nivel medio del agua

Nivel mínimo del agua

Fondo de la laguna

Sección D-D

N Pabellones temporales
   sobre balsas flotantes.

I Pilares sustentantes de señales,
   carteles de información.

...es, kioskos, café - Restaurante
...a exposición.

J Balcón-mirador
   sobre el agua.

K Rampa-puente ajustable automáticamente
   a los cambios de nivel de agua, la pendiente
   máxima de 10 grados permite el acceso
   a los minusválidos.

L Poste de amarre

M Pontones metálicos flotantes, encadenados para
   facilitar acceso a los pabellones temporales.

203.

FRANKFURT ZOO
FRANKFURT, WEST GERMANY

The 160 acre Frankfurt Zoo is conceived as a succession of natural habitats, in which landscape and architecture are integrated into an organic whole.

The location of the different animal habitats is designed to maintain typological affinities between animal herds. The habitats are also organized in topographical sequence, so that the forest habitat blends gradually into that of the bush, and so on, with an eventual return to the forest.

Animal herds are kept separate from one another and from visitors by means of natural barriers such as waterways, ditches, berms, and other devices that conceal fences from visitors' view. Where glass is used to separate animals from humans, shade coverings above the glass minimize reflections so that the glass becomes an almost invisible membrane. The animals' enclosures blend into the landscape of their habitats, minimizing stress on the animals, and offering visitors the most realistic depiction possible for the animals' natural environments.

In order to help visitors orient themselves as easily as possible, circulation through the zoo is organized into two different routes that are defined by concentric rings: the inner route, or "Short Journey," and the other route, or "Long Journey." Those who wish to stay only a short time can follow the inner ring, along which are located the zoo's most popular inhabitants. Visitors planning a more leisurely tour can follow the outer ring. Both routes, however, include a stop at the central "Paradise," a metaphorical Garden of Eden populated by flying, walking, and swinging animals that live in a sylvan valley of rocks, caves, ponds, and waterfalls. The paths of the long and short journeys, as well as the short branch walkways connecting them, follow a constantly undulating line, to keep visitors from running into one another, thereby minimizing crowding and maximizing the sense that one is alone with the animals in their natural setting.

In contrast to the emphasis on natural habitats for the animals, all buildings used by human visitors are clearly architectural creations, identified by rows of columns. The zoo's two entrances—one from the subway and the other from the parking lot—are connected by a colonnade that helps orient visitors to the lecture hall and the restaurant at the main visitors' building.

The organization of the zoo's service system insures that service roads never cross pedestrian paths. The main service road runs along the perimeter of the zoo, slightly below the level of the animal habitats and out of the visitors' view. The main service area, which includes the animal hospital, is located at the northernmost tip of the site, in a man-made lower level that is hidden from sight by the zebras' savanna habitat. This location allows for future expansion of the zoo to the west.

ZO
FRANKF

Große Stepp

Große Stepp

1 3 0 6

Legende

Übersicht

Paradiso

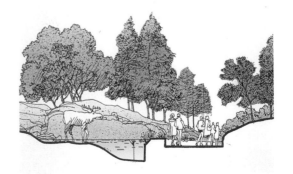

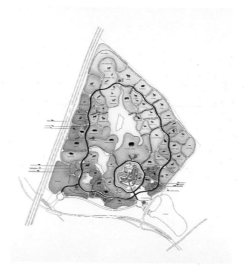

NICHII OBIHIRO DEPARTMENT STORE
OBIHIRO, JAPAN

This department store will be built in Obihiro, the second largest city on Hokkaido, Japan's northernmost island. Climatically similar to Siberia, Hokkaido's ever-present image is that of a winter in which snow seems somehow to fall horizontally. The Mycal Group, owner of the Nichii department store in Obihiro, is an enlightened corporation, committed to the notion that customers should be treated as old friends; it is their responsibility as merchants to provide a pleasant, welcoming environment. This department store, therefore, will offer the citizens of Obihiro a grand wintergarden, where people can gather under a glass sky-light to look at plants, listen to water cascades, and stroll along walkways in the courtyard around which the building is organized.

The store will be dedicated not only to retail sales, but also to various other services, ranging from health clubs and restaurants to mountain-climbing lessons. This unusual variety of services results from the Japanese policy that forbids department stores from competing directly with smaller shops, and which allows them to expand only if they provide services as well as retail goods. The store will also house micro-factories for baking, wine bottling, knitting, and garment assembly, and will contain hotels, banquet halls, and even wedding chapels. In this way, the store will also address the city's lack of space for large social gatherings.

Since the store covers approximately two-and-a-half acres (a rather large footprint for a Japanese build-ing), the client wanted the building to present the friendliest possible face to the community. Therefore, the store is "covered" with greenery. In fact, the building has an outer layer of glass, but the space between it and the insulated walls of the building container is filled with plants. Visitors driving around the building will see it from all sides as a naturally green promonotory, rising from an earthen podium that conceals ex-tensive underground parking facilities. The building's faceted glass walls rise to a peak; their irregular shape dictated by sun and shade angles, as well as by zoning and height limitations and the presence of a mi-crowave beam carrying telephone communications 33 meters above the ground. As visitors enter the building, they will discover that this promonotory also has a green heart that pulses with springtime, even in the middle of winter.

UNION STATION
KANSAS CITY, MISSOURI

This proposal for the re-use of Union Station attempts to preserve a great building of the past by making it an urbanistically and economically vital part of the community.

The key urban design element of the project ties Union Station to the magnificent green carpet of Liberty Park, from which it is now cut off by Pershing Avenue, a busy thoroughfare. Taking advantage of the 80-foot drop from the park's Liberty Memorial to the station, the hillside will be extended over a new, above-ground tunnel over Pershing Avenue, and down to the station's entrance. To the east, a small footbridge will connect the park to nearby Crown Center. Thus, Liberty Park would become an impressive and appropriate frontspiece to the station, reconnecting it to the surroundings from which, through urban growth, it has become isolated.

The park "continues" into the former station's vast public areas, turning them in to wintergardens. The areas of the building flanking these central wintergardens will be adapted to serve cultural functions that would support the building.

The Grand Hall, once the station's waiting room, will be transformed in to a botanical conservatory, illuminated by winter sun through its south-facing windows. Rather than obscure the hall's elegant architecture with plantings, the conservatory will be located in a series of stepped terraces set in a "quarry" created by cutting 50 feet down into the floor of the 96-foot-high space. Use as a wintergarden will drastically reduce heating and cooling costs, making the space an economic asset rather than a liability. The conservatory will serve as the main entrance to the east and west wings, which flank the Grand Hall and will house a proposed aquarium and an art museum, respectively. Open to these two conventionally heated and cooled wings, the conservatory's temperature would be moderated by the continuous influx of conditioned air.

The almost 400-foot-long north wing will house the second of the building's two wintergardens on its upper level. A neoclassical garden room, in the tradition of Longwood Gardens in Delaware, it will serve both civic and trade gatherings. An enclosed cafe at the room's entrance will provide comfortable seating, while a grotto at the room's far end will conceal the roof of a proposed Omnimax theater. The lower level of the north wing, where the station's platforms and tracks were located, will house a transportation museum.

A refurbished carriage house on the station's west side will serve as a group entrance for the art museum and will also house a planetarium. To the east, the building will have its own stop on a proposed light rapid transit system.

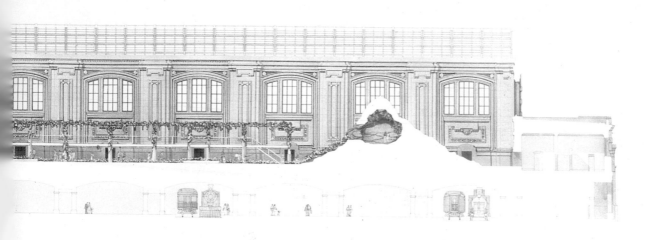

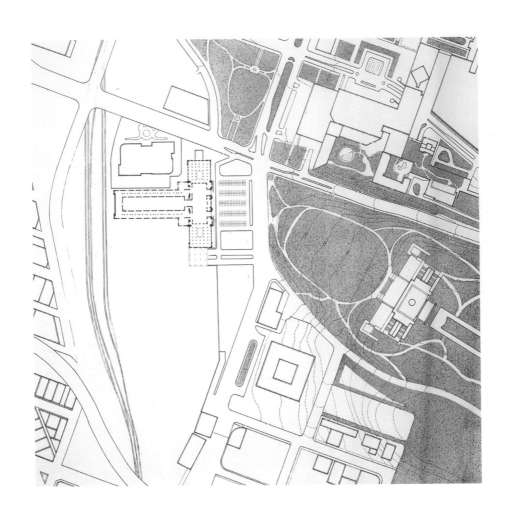

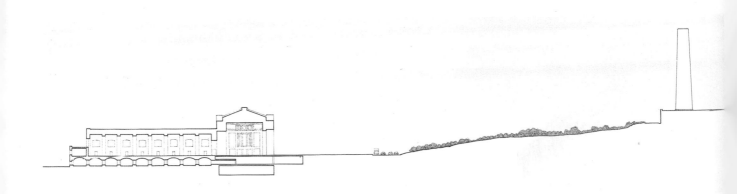

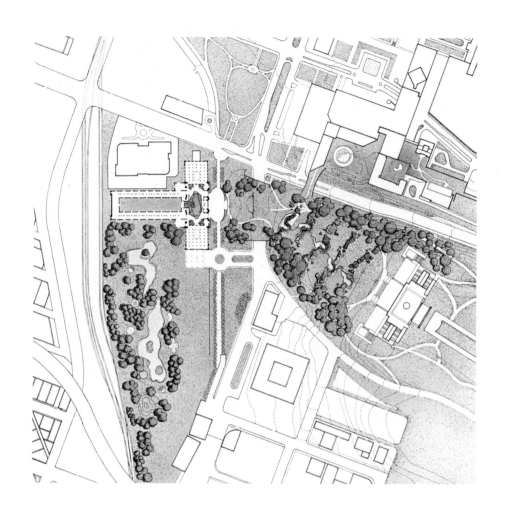

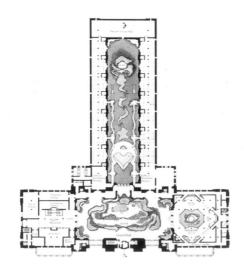

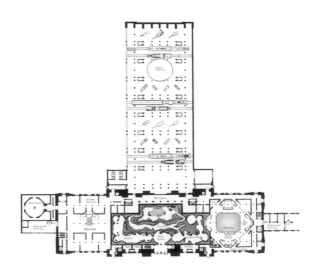

Exhibit Design

Italy: The New Domestic Landscape

The Chairs Of Charles Rennie Mackintosh

The Taxi Project

Exhibit Design
Museum of Modern Art, New York, 1970–1976

ITALY: THE NEW DOMESTIC LANDSCAPE, 1972 (pp. 227–231), consisted of more than 150 objects, each an example of the outstanding design produced in Italy since 1960. The exhibit was notable for its use of an exterior venue and for the "crates" which served as containers for the objects. On one level, the crates answered the functional problems of a traveling show; the movable doors projected shadows during the summer when raised for display, and when lowered, sealed each container for shipping. On a second level, the crates created a micro urban environment, providing the public with shopping avenues that seduce with their views of designed artifacts.

THE CHAIRS OF CHARLES RENNIE MACKINTOSH, 1974 (pp. 232–235), presented a collection of the Scottish architect's chairs along with some of his graphic work and original drawings. Photographs showing the chairs in their original settings were also included.

The gallery walls were painted a dark purple-gray, the richness, not the color, being the important element. Through the use of color and lighting, the installation attempted to suggest an ambience reminiscent of the spaces Mackintosh created, without resorting to historical mimicry that would have competed with the exhibition's primary intention: the presentation of the designed object as an art form complete in itself. The elaborate chairs were spotlighted to create dramatic shadows. The remainder were arranged chronologically and backlighted by fixtures filtered through a double layer of voile fabric which created a moire pattern suggestive of art nouveau ornamentation.

THE TAXI PROJECT, 1976 (pp. 236–239), was organized to address the inability of available taxis to answer the requirements of urban transportation. Various international manufacturers were invited to participate, and a manual of engineering specifications was developed to ensure consistency of response to the design brief.

The resulting prototypes were displayed on two intersecting "streets," defined by "curbs" of rubber matting on which technical data was silk-screened. Overhead lights were both lowered and dimmed as they receded from the viewer, effectively creating the feeling of vanishing perspective. The walls of the exhibition space were painted to resemble an abstract cityscape in early evening, complete with "billboards" onto which were projected constantly changing images illustrating how the different taxis could be used by the general public—people with luggage, the handicapped, etc.

Proposals for street furniture, including benches, waiting stations and electronic display systems were also presented, suggesting possible design directions for this secondary, but equally important, aspect of the transportation experience.

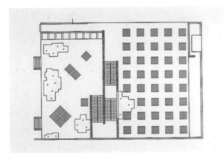

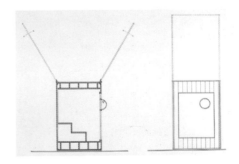

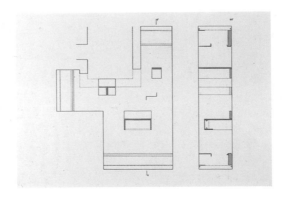

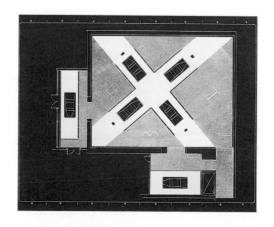

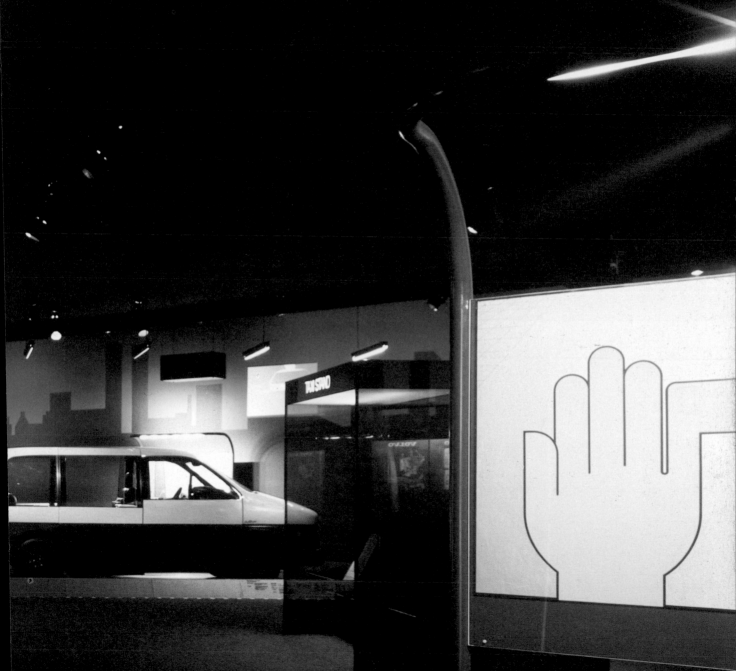

Industrial Design

Vertebra

Dorsal

Lumb-R

L-System

N-14

Escargot

Logotec

Oseris

Agamennone

Soffio

Skelton

Toothbrushes

Vittel Water Bottle

Aquacolor

Polyphemus

Delilah

Vertebra, 1974 (pp. 243–251). When working at their desks, people shift back and forth, looking for a momentarily comfortable position. This slumping and stretching is the body's natural response to uncomplimentary seating; the muscles want to relax so the sitter moves about. The Vertebra seating system recognizes this problem, and shapes its design from it. Vertebra behaves like we do, as organisms in motion. Whether we lean forward or back, the chair goes with us.

Since the ideal chair requires no adjustment whatsoever, Vertebra changes its configuration gently and automatically. It accepts the fact that our bodies are composed of an intricate combination of bones, muscles, blood vessels, flesh, and nerves. And since people rarely stay in the same seated position for more than ten minutes, Vertebra is designed to keep up with the sitter's every movement—without the use of buttons, levers or mechanisms.

The original Vertebra seating form has now been systematically developed into a range of side and arm chairs outfitted for operational, managerial, and executive needs.

Dorsal, 1978 (pp. 252–255), designed as an economical institutional chair, provides instant adaptability to the myriad range of sitting needs of the contemporary office worker. Like Vertebra, but less expensive, Dorsal was created with the idea in mind that a chair must function not only ergonomically, but also as a cultural artifact.

Employing ergonomic and orthopedic research in its automatically functioning backrest and in its overall configuration of interrelated parts, Dorsal relaxes the sitter's body. The chair "disappears" during use, becoming a moving part of the worker.

Lumb-R Seating, 1980 (pp. 256–257), designed originally as a sturdy, attractive line of articulated seating at a price-point similar to non-articulated chairs then on the market, continues to satisfy the needs of the seated office worker. Since many such office workers must lean over their desk for extended periods of time, they very commonly develop lower back or lumbar-region spinal pain.

Targeted for organizations where work such as this frequently occurs, LUMB-R incorporates orthopedic considerations into its seat and cut-out backrest design. Additionally, all edges on the chair have been rounded to permit maximum blood circulation, and all possible projections from the chair have been eliminated. Like Vertebra and Dorsal, all LUMB-R's adjustments to movement are automatic. Because of this, LUMB-R makes all seating postures ideal. As the sitter moves back, the center of gravity shifts with him, and back-muscle strain is relieved. LUMB-R's optimal weight distribution and lumbar support insures the worker's comfort, and in so doing, increases the possibility for efficient and productive work.

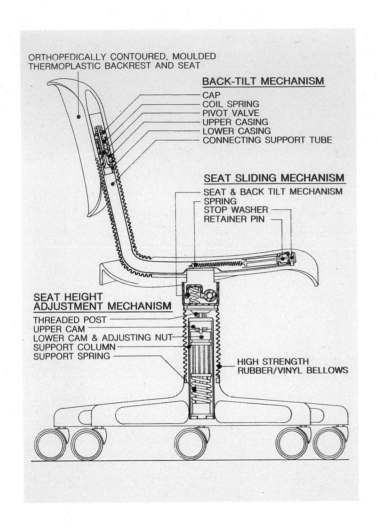

ORTHOPEDICALLY CONTOURED, MOULDED
THERMOPLASTIC BACKREST AND SEAT

BACK-TILT MECHANISM
CAP
COIL SPRING
PIVOT VALVE
UPPER CASING
LOWER CASING
CONNECTING SUPPORT TUBE

SEAT SLIDING MECHANISM
SEAT & BACK TILT MECHANISM
SPRING
STOP WASHER
RETAINER PIN

**SEAT HEIGHT
ADJUSTMENT MECHANISM**
THREADED POST
UPPER CAM
LOWER CAM & ADJUSTING NUT
SUPPORT COLUMN
SUPPORT SPRING

HIGH STRENGTH
RUBBER/VINYL BELLOWS

upright

relax

tilt forward

tilt backward

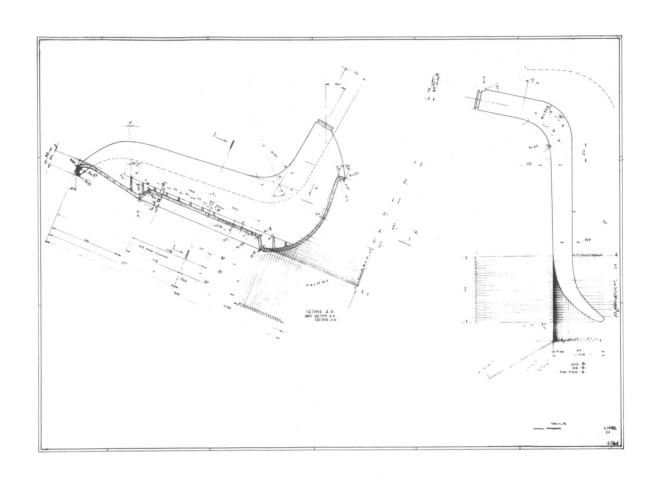

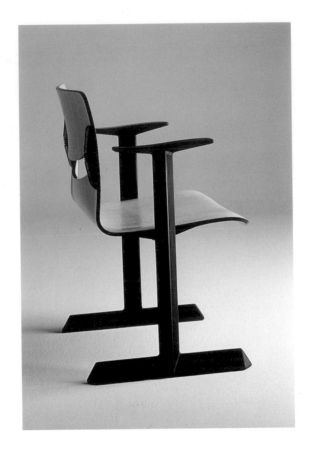

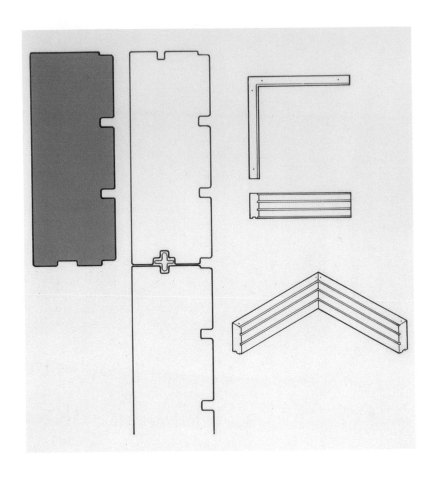

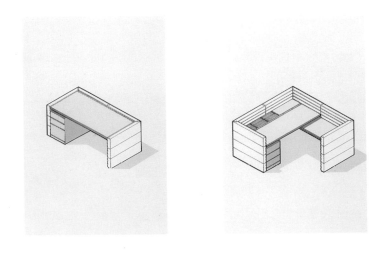

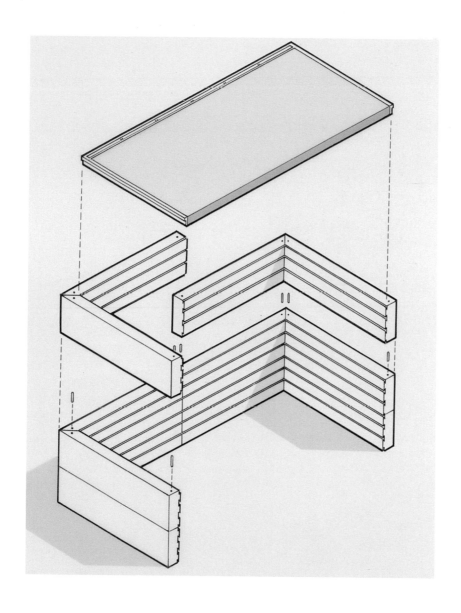

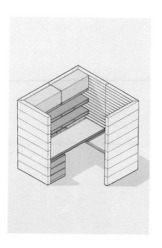

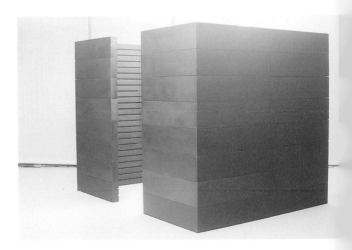

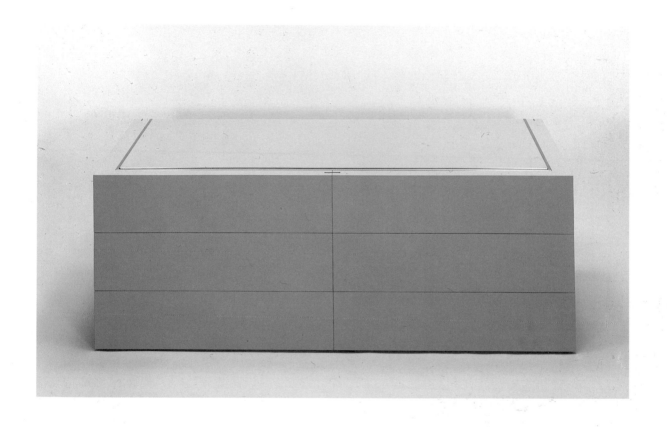

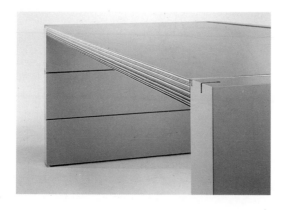

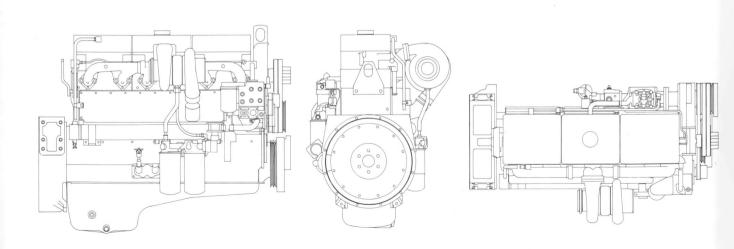

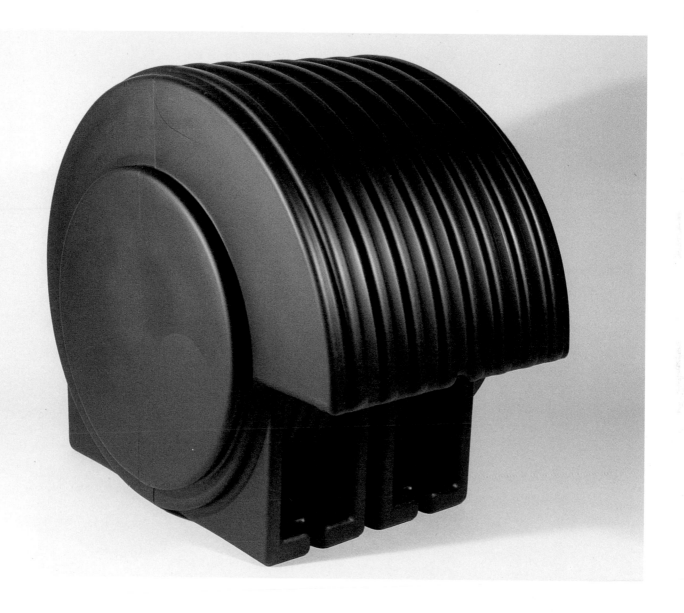

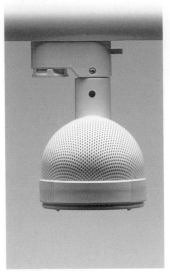

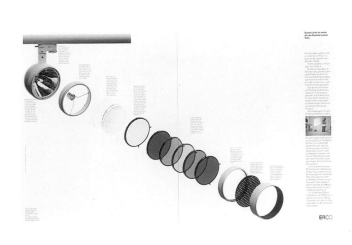

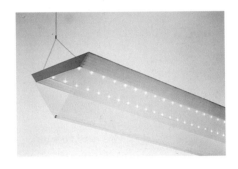

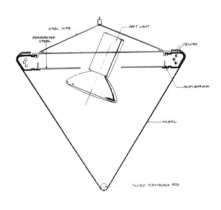

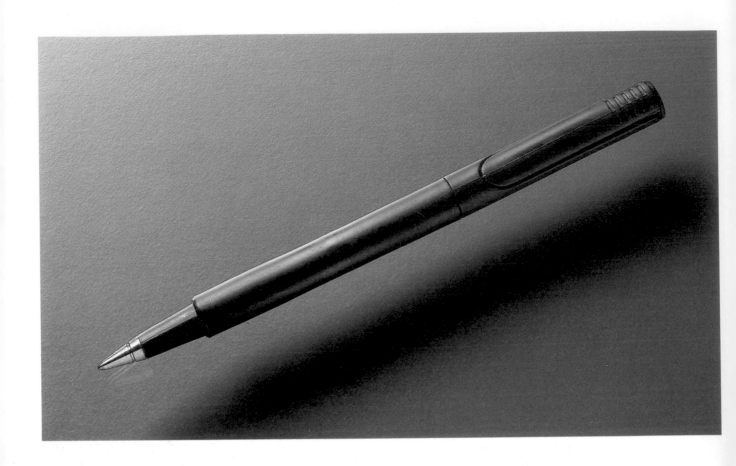

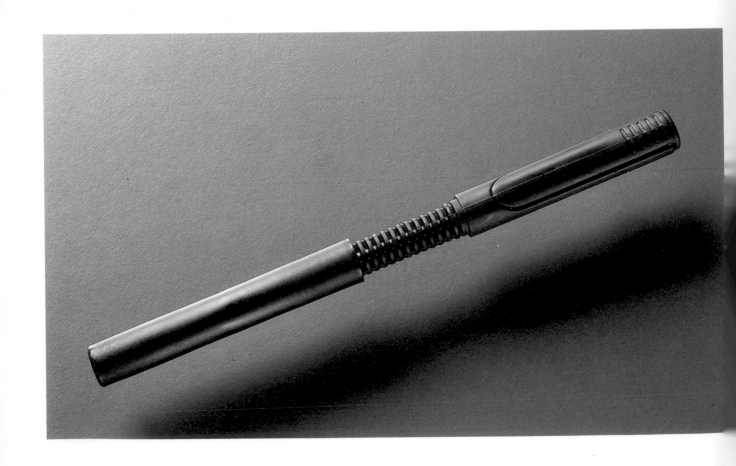

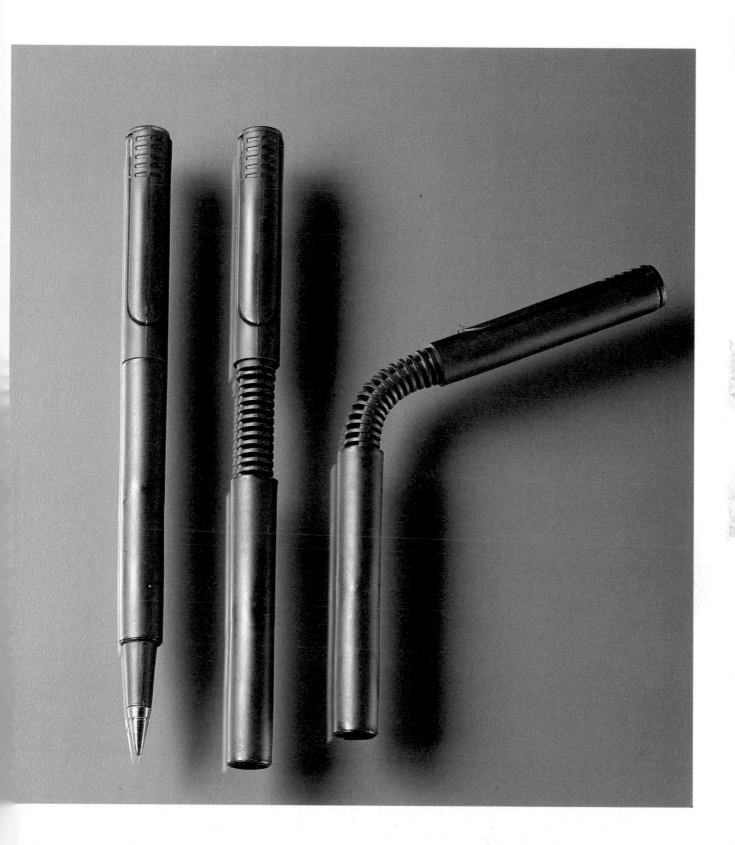

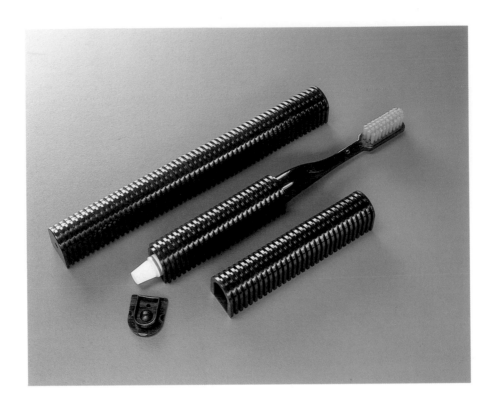

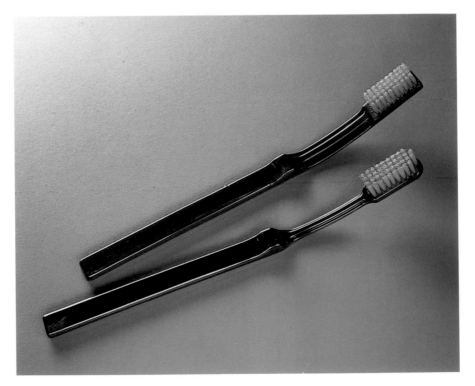

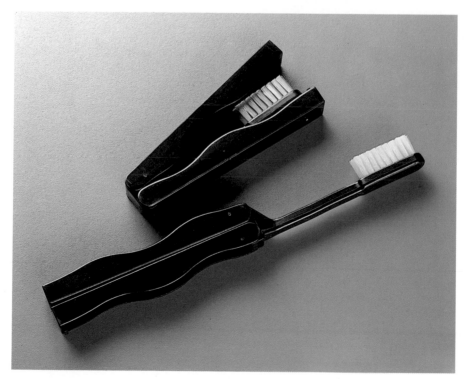

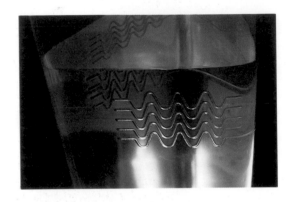

COMPOSITION in mg liter

Bicarbonates	357	Nitrates	
Calcium	78	Chlorides	
Magnesium	24	Potassium	
Sulphates	10	Fluorides	4.2
Sodium	5		

*SALT FREE
(only 1.2 mg per 8 oz glass)

Product of France

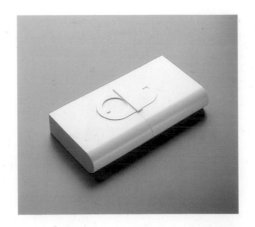

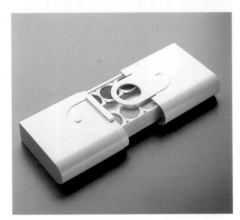

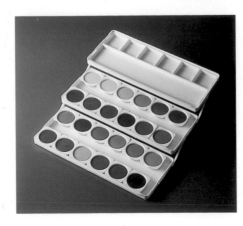

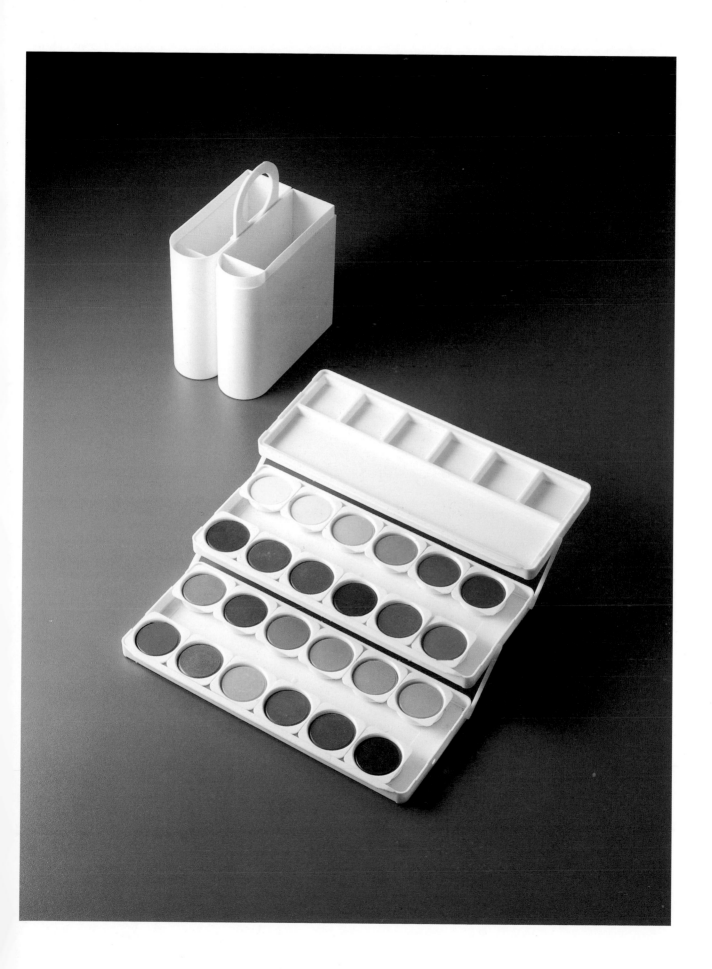

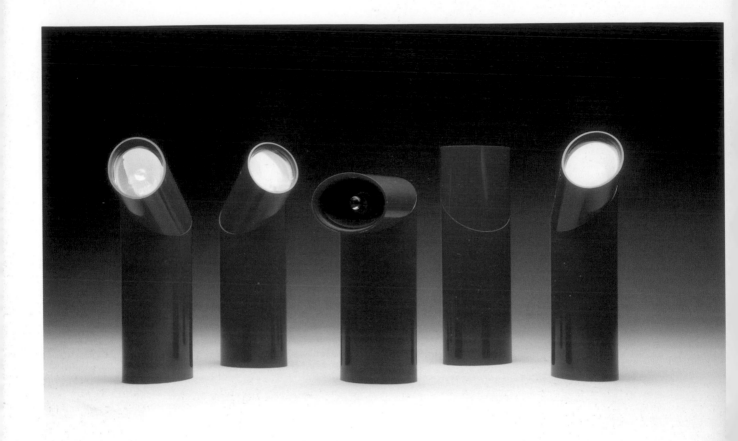

L-SYSTEM, 1973 (pp. 258–263) is based on a single, structural L-shaped unit that acts as the fundamental building block for a modular furniture system. With L-System pieces, arrangements for either the office or the residence can be created. It is possible to link units together to form a sofa, to stack units to form shelving, or to organize L-Systems into work stations or even multi-seating areas. Anti-erector set in concept, L-System eliminates the need for costly, easily lost sets of pieces and parts. Instead, L-system uses only the smallest group of pins necessary to insure that horizontal displacement does not occur.

N14 LITER AUTOMOTIVE/INDUSTRIAL DIESEL ENGINE, 1982 (pp. 264–265), features a revolutionary new oil cooling technique which extends the engine's operating period to major overhaul from 500,000 to 800,000 miles. This new cooling technique also allows a reduction in engine weight by 550 lbs. per engine, resulting in enhanced savings for the manufacturer, Cummins Engine.

The N14 engine, with models ranging from 300 to 450 HP, achieves major improvements in fuel economy, noise reduction, durability and emissions while retaining enough commonality with current N type engines to permit use of much of Cummins existing tooling and transfer lines. The arrangement of Turbo charger, after-cooler and cross-over on one side of the engine has resulted in a height reduction of 9 inches, allowing it to fit a greater range of vehicles.

The cylinder block and valve covers have been designed to express power and denote structural strength, and the engine's dark blue and black color has been developed to emphasize ruggedness and to hide production imperfections.

ESCARGOT AIR FILTER, 1985 (pp. 266–267), designed for use with large industrial engines, such as diesel engines or electrical generators, integrates its plastic housing with the actual air filter of the unit. By molding the entire Escargot unit integrally, and by making it out of plastic which requires no painting, a great savings in manufacture is realized. Self-contained and having no movable parts, Escargot is essentially a cartridge filter. When its life is exhausted, it is simply replaced, unlike other units on the market. In this way, Escargot ensures that an expensive engine will not be damaged by dirt or dust getting into it when the filter is being changed (as is also the case with conventional non-disposable filters).

Escargot is not only named after the snail, it takes its functional clues from it as well. The air inlet—the opening of the snail and the point of entry into the filter—offers a very efficient way of distributing air into and through the filtering surfaces. While its appearance is the direct result of functional requirements, the snail-like configuration also operates at a higher level; it is emblematic of an in-out process during which a transformation takes place.

Logotec, 1980 (pp. 268–269). Designed for the contract and institutional lighting field, Logotec allows for very fine lighting adjustments. From simple controls to complex operations such as color corrections and image framing, Logotec combines general service lamps with powerful reflectors and two fitting sizes to create an integrated whole. By using such general service lamps, re-lamping costs are also kept low.

Formed by cutting a circular cylinder at a 45-degree angle, the two basic fittings, backed by a very small number of accessories, are capable of meeting all lighting requirements. Camera-like in its detail, Logotec allows the user to calibrate precisely the direction in which the light is being aimed.

Oseris, 1982 (pp. 270–271), a range of low-voltage, high-wattage spotlights, is named for the Egyptian god of ancient mythology. Through the combination of two different small size, low energy consumption quartz halogen lamps with a comprehensive collection of accessories, Oseris works as a system, which also includes ceiling mountings, flood lenses, honeycomb screens, infra-red reflecting filters, multi-groove baffles, sculpture lenses, and fixing rings for both colored glass filters and anti-dazzle cylinders. Future lamps and accessories will also fit into this range, giving Oseris a much longer product life span than other spotlights.

By using 20W to 100W lamps, Oseris uses energy more efficiently and reduces heat load in the process. Oseris is also based on the fact that the intersections of a semi-spherical volume twice cut with a plane generate perfect circles. These two circles are then turned one against the other, describing a movement from 0 to 90 degrees. Additionally, Oseris can rotate 360 degrees on its vertical axis. To assist in optimal alignment of lighting, scales are imprinted on the light fixture, allowing precise illumination when multiple fittings are placed in a row, as in museum and gallery installations.

Agamennone, 1985 (pp. 272–273), named after the ancient Greek king, is a black floor lamp based on twice cutting an elliptical cylinder at a 45-degree angle to yield two perfect circles. These two circles rotate against each other from a single, shared circumferential point—always at a right angle to each other—and allow a range of motion that extends through a full 360 degrees. Unlike other lamps, which operate within a single plane (or two at the most), Agamennone's head travels along a circular path through respective "X," "Y," and "Z" axes. Driven by two miniature electric motors, the head's rotation can be operated either manually or through a hand-held remote control, providing a high degree of lighting freedom.

Agamennone employs current technology to maximum advantage by using a metal halide bulb that produces higher luminosity with less electricity, and which has a life span three times greater than standard bulbs. At ease in almost any environment, its minimal contemporary form and color are balanced by its reduced electrical consumption and longevity.

Soffio, 1986 (pp. 274–277), is an economical yet highly versatile modular lighting system designed for contract and residential interiors. While most such systems are unamiably high tech, Soffio has a softer side that utilizes sophisticated technologies without jarring, hard edges.

By using two lighting track channels, one suitable for 110V and the other for 12/24V, and by using the same lighting tray to support light sources that can shine upwards, downwards, or both ways, Soffio creates unique lighting advantages. With it, for example, fluorescent tubes can be combined or interchanged with halogen and/or filament bulbs to intensify floor light as well as accent desired areas.

The key to Soffio is that it shields its fixtures and aluminum channel tracks with a gauzy, self-extinguishing, washable, iridescent synthetic fabric. No matter which fixture is employed, the light has a warm, human quality, with reduced glare and subtle tonalities. Soffio, which means a wafting breeze in Italian, is a lightweight, organic lighting system whose design is based on merging the qualities of light with the diverse needs of institutional illumination. Simple in its installation and in its maintenance, the system offers a soft presence in what is normally the hard-tech world of the contemporary office.

Skelton, 1986 (pp. 278–279), an economical, soft and flexible ballpoint pen, is easier than most pens to carry in coat, shirt, or pants pockets. Based on the observation that children and adults alike often have pens break in their pockets and spoil their clothes, the pen softly and naturally follows the body's contours.

Skelton is intrinsically comfortable, able to bend a full 90 degrees. When its middle is unscrewed, the pen becomes elastic and agile, and when it is retracted, the pen stiffens and becomes easy to guide. The pen utilizes a full-length refill capable of writing for at least a mile, and has a permanently attached cap, eliminating the "lost cap" problem.

Skelton immediately conveys its nimble characteristics; its shape signifies its flexibility, and in turn gives the user the feeling that some small magic is used as an ordinary object becomes a momentary enchantment.

Toothbrushes, 1987 (pp. 280–281). Reflecting current trends in personal oral hygiene and utilizing advances in brush and bristle design, these toothbrushes have been designed to meet a wide range of contemporary needs, including portability. A purse-size toothbrush is designed for women, a pair of toothbrushes that share the same geometry (but have differing details) is designed for a couple, and a toothbrush that changes the angle of its head to conform to tooth surfaces and a pocket-size folding model are for everybody.

VITTEL WATER BOTTLE, 1986 (pp. 282–283). The Vittel water bottle is based on water itself, and a merging of the bottle's practical requirements with the substance's sensual delights. The water bottle has a feeling of quality, of a clean and elegant ascetic package. It is easy to grip, and has been envisioned and tested to feel good in the hand. By integrating texture into the blow-molding manufacturing process, the Vittel bottle is also not slippery. This texture, which looks like a wavy "V," suggests both the company name and the ripples of water; this characteristic has particular importance for marketing reasons as product identity is strengthened through multiple association.

The bottle suggests that water is a wondrous commodity. It pours smoothly from the mouth of the bottle, and bottles can be stacked on top of each other or packaged in groups of seven to form a circle for a week's worth of drinking. Like a perfume container for water, the bottle is designed to signal that something of real quality is inside.

AQUACOLOR, 1987 (pp. 284–285), an updating of the classic water color set, consists of a three-tiered, hinged palette with color trays that can easily be removed for cleaning or replacement. The two halves of its self-locking storage and carrying case have been designed to function additionally as a segmented water bucket, reducing the number of objects required in order to paint.

Innovative in its concern for the problems of cleaning, storage, and usage with respect to both adult and children painters, the Aquacolor box is easy to carry, empty, and maintain, and provides a distinctive product identity. It leaves the rusted tin box far behind, and costs only a few cents more than the earlier model.

DELILAH, 1985 (pp. 286–287), originally designed for Philips, is shaped to provide the user with the greatest ease and comfort while shaving. The head, cut at 45 degrees to the body of the shaver, rotates freely through the "X", "Y," and "Z" axes, allowing the cutting blades optimal positioning without requiring awkward or uncomfortable wrist or hand movements. Due to its rotating head, Delilah, in addition to advancing the ergonomics of shaver design, requires little room and can be easily packed for travel.

POLYPHEMUS, 1985 (pp. 288–289), is based on sectioning an elliptical cylinder at a 45 degree angle to create a circle, on which a rotating flashlight head turns. By bending the flashlight into an L-configuration, it can easily be carried, and it is ergonomically more comfortable to the hand and wrist in such a position.

Built from separate male and female parts snapped together, the flashlight can stand or lay on any surface while its light beam is aimed in any direction. Additionally, it holds a magnet inside so that it can be attached to a metal surface. The unique shape of the flashlight utilizes a patented topological principle that suggests a number of consumer end-uses.

Graphic Design

Confessional Notes About My Work

World Man: Bucky Fuller Poster

Geigy Graphics Poster

Surface and Ornament Poster

Axis Poster

Italy: The New Domestic Landscape Poster

Italy: The New Domestic Landscape Book Cover

Mimar

Taxi Project Book Cover

Barcelona Chair Postcard

Residence Au Lac Card

Personal Stationery

Bank Bruxelles Lambert, New York Card

Seeds Greeting Card

Calendar Memory Bags

Diary File Agenda

Memo-Plan Agenda

Mycal Group Identity

Chiocciola

Graphic Design
Confessional Notes About My Work

In truth, I do not make graphic designs. I make objects, either buildings or products, some of which just happen to be made of paper. Occasionally I create symbols, such as the taxi exhibition logotype, or lay out a poster, like the one for Geigy; but even then, I must confess, I envision them more as three-dimensional objects than simply as printed pieces. I do so, perhaps, out of fascination with the inner life of matter. I have a surrealist's obsession with the infinitesimal space between two sheets of paper and with the actual thickness of the paper itself. I perceive paper as a mass contained between two facades. For these reasons, I see paper as an architectonic material with two attributes: it is a shield suggesting what is behind it, and, at the same time, it is a volume so soft that a design may dwell inside.

As for my attitude toward problem solving in graphic design, I can distinguish between two features of my work. First, I try, not always successfully, to go beyond the problem at hand. Take, for example, the calendar-memory bag. It can be used like any straightforward calendar. But since paper possesses for me an inner space—and because I believe that a calendar should not only help us plan for what is to come (l'avenir) but also help us hold onto whatever we wish to keep from the past (le souvenir)—I have conceived this calendar so that one can keep within it things one wishes to collect: recipes, newspaper clippings, laundry and lottery tickets, baby's snapshots, fallen leaves, and the like. It also offers the possibility of tearing off any bad day one wishes to forget while still maintaining the overall structure of the month.

The second aspect of my approach to problem solving is that, being lazy, I always look around to see whether something does not already exist that I can reuse. In the case of the calendar, I reutilized both interoffice envelopes and brown paper grocery bags. Since I feel slightly guilty, however, for having thus betrayed our forefathers' blind trust in progress, and their belief in new products as the healers of mankind's problems, I have felt compelled to develop a philosophical theory to justify such behavior.

world man bucky fuller

mc cosh 10
october 5
8 p. m.

princeton university school of architecture

Geigy Graphics on exhibition april 1967
princeton university   school of architecture

Geigy Graphics on exhibition april 1967
princeton university   school of architecture

Geigy Graphics on exhibition april 1967
princeton university   school of architecture

Geigy Graphics on exhibition april 1967
princeton university school of architecture

Surface & Ornament

Formica Corporation invites you to submit entries in its two COLORCORE™ "Surface & Ornament" design competitions in 1983-84.

COLORCORE laminate is a new surfacing material from Formica Corporation. It is the first laminate with integral solid color. This feature eliminates the dark line associated with laminate applications. Additionally, dimensional and graphic effects are possible with routed channels which remain the same color as the surface.

"Surface & Ornament" is composed of two independent competitions which invite the design community to explore the potential of COLORCORE. Over $80,000 in prizes will be awarded. Judging will be based on overall excellence, technique and inventiveness in demonstrating the unique characteristics of COLORCORE. Colors are limited to original 12 COLORCORE colorways in Competition I.

COMPETITION I (CONCEPTUAL): Open to all architects, designers, fabricators and students, with students having their own category. The purpose is to design an object no larger than 64 cubic feet surfaced with COLORCORE. Designs can be either residential or commercial including such items as TV cabinets, office work stations, dining tables or any decorative or useful object. Prizes are as follows: Professionals—1st Prize $10,000; 2nd Prize $5,000; 3rd Prize $2,000; 4th Prize $1,000. Students—1st Prize $5,000 plus a $5,000 contribution to the student's school. Citations will also be awarded.

Scale models of winning entries will be built and exhibited during NEOCON XV, along with invited designs by

the following prominent designers and architects: Emilio Ambasz, Ward Bennett, Frank O. Gehry, Milton Glaser, Helmut Jahn, Charles W. Moore, Stanley Tigerman, Venturi, Rauch and Scott Brown, Massimo and Lella Vignelli and SITE Inc.

Publication of the designs and a traveling exhibit of winning projects are also planned.

Judges are: Charles Boxenbaum, Joe D'Urso, Paul Segal, William Turnbull from Formica Corporation's Design Advisory Board. Other judges are: Niels Diffrient, industrial designer; David Gebhard, University of California, Santa Barbara; and Robert Maxwell, Dean, School of Architecture, Princeton University.

Entries must be postmarked by February 15, 1983. Judging will take place March 15, 1983. Winners will be notified by April 1 and publicly announced at NEOCON XV. For deadline and full details, please write Formica Corporation immediately.

COMPETITION II (BUILT): Open to all professional architects and designers for completed room installations, and in-production product designs utilizing COLORCORE. Prizes are as follows: In each of three categories—Product Design, Residential and Contract installations: 1st Prizes of $15,000 and 2nd Prizes of $5,000. Citations will also be awarded.

Judges are: Alan Buchsbaum and John Saladino from Formica Corporation's Design Advisory Board. Other judges are: Jack Lenor Larsen, James Stewart Polshek, Dean, School of Architecture, Columbia University;

Andrée Putman, interior designer; Laurinda Spear, Arquitectonica; Robert A.M. Stern.

Documentation of completed work must be submitted in a series of 35mm slides with complete description of project and why COLORCORE was used. Current projects are eligible. Judging will take place March 15, 1984. For deadline and full details, please write Formica Corporation.

DEADLINES TIMETABLE	COMPETITION I	COMPETITION II
Earliest date for mailing entries	10-15-82	3-1-83
Last postmark date for mailing of inquiries	12-31-82	12-1-83
LAST POSTMARK DATE FOR MAILING ENTRIES	2-15-83	2-15-84
Jury Convenes	3-15-83	3-15-84
Announcements To Winners (confidentially)	4-1-83	4-2-84
To Public	NEOCON XV	NEOCON XVI
Exhibitions	NEOCON XV	NEOCON XVI

For free samples, call toll-free number 1-800-543-3000. Ask for Operator #375. In Ohio call: 1-800-582-1396.

Entrants are strongly urged to call for "Rules and Regulations" manual and samples.

Address entries or requests for information to: COLORCORE "Surface and Ornament" Competition, Formica Corporation, One Cyanamid Plaza, Wayne, N.J. 07470.

EMILIO AMBASZ

ARCHITECTURAL • INDUSTRIAL • GRAPHIC • EXHIBIT DESIGN

April 16, 1985 to May 6, 1985

AXIS
4F AXIS Building
5-17-1, Roppongi
Minato-ku, Tokyo.

1985年4月16日（火）より5月6日（月）まで
11:00AM〜6:00PM（最終日3:00PM）
入場無料

アクシスギャラリー（アクシスビル4F）
東京都港区六本木5-17-1
TEL.03(587)2781

ORGANIZER
AXIS

PATRONS
Embassy of the United States of America
Argentine Embassy
Italian embassy
The International Council of
The Museum of Modern Art

COLLABORATOR
Bridgestone

COOPERATORS
INAX
Shokubutsu
Toray Industries
Nuno
7L Yamagiwa Laboratory

Argentine born Emilio Ambasz is very active in
various fields as architect, industrial designer,
graphic designer and curator. His New York
office engages mainly in architectural projects,
whose innovative technology and lyrical qualities
have won him many awards and worldwide
recognition. In addition to acting as Chief Design
Consultant for Cummins Engine Company, a company
renown for its enlightened support of architecture
and design, Mr. Ambasz maintains an office in
Bologna, Italy's combination of traditional
craftsmanship and sophisticated engineering has
enabled him to design as well as develop a number of
industrial products, ranging from furniture to lighting
and electronic equipment. A writer of articles and
books, Mr. Ambasz is also active in cultural endeavors
related to architecture and design both as former
Curator of Design at the Museum of Modern
Art (NYC) and as current President of The Architectural
League.

エミリオ・アンバースはアルゼンチンに生まれ、
建築家、工業デザイナー、グラフィックデザイナ
ー、キュレーターとして多くの領域で精力的
な活動をしている。彼はニューヨークの事務所
で主に建築のプロジェクトに従事し、革新
的な技術と詩的な質により、数々の賞と世界
的な評価を得ている。そして、建築やデザイン
を積極的に支援する美しい企業として知られるカミ
ンズエンジン社のデザインコンサルタントとして
も活動している。またイタリアのボローニャに事務所
を持ち、イタリアの伝統的な職人芸と洗練され
た工業技術により、家具から照明器具や電気
製品までの、数多くの影響力のある製品の開発、
デザインをおこなっている。現在、アンバース氏
はニューヨーク近代美術館の元デザ
イン部門キュレーターとして、また建築
や本の著述をも含めて、建築やデザイン部門で
の文化的な貢献をしている。

主催
アクシス

後援
アメリカ大使館
アルゼンチン大使館
イタリア大使館
ニューヨーク近代美術館国際協議会

協賛
ブリヂストン

協力
イナックス
シトーキ
東レ
布
7L ヤマギワ研究所

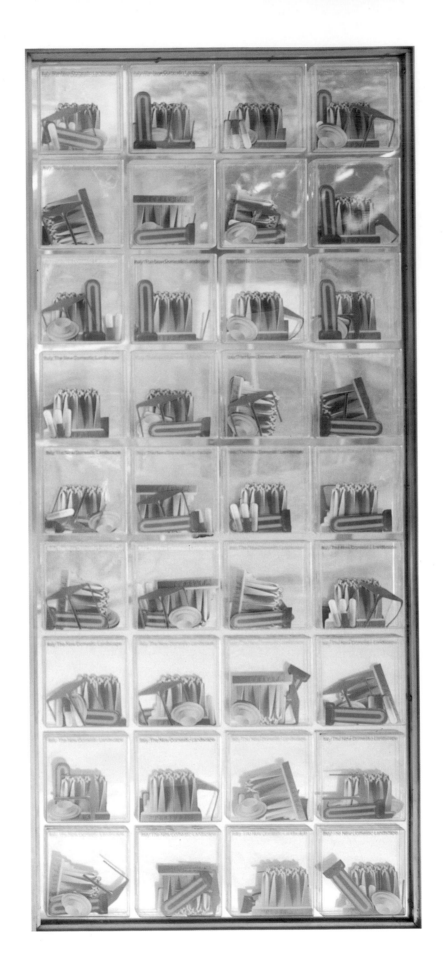

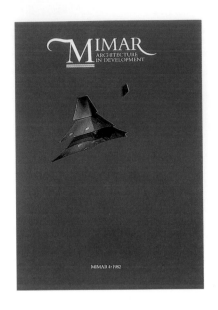

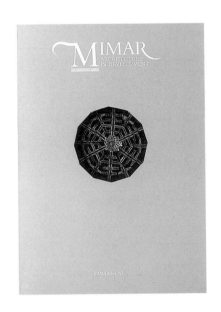

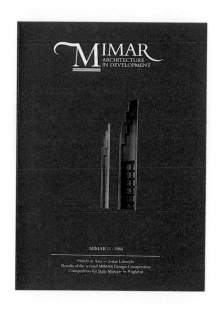

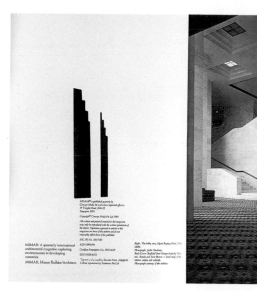

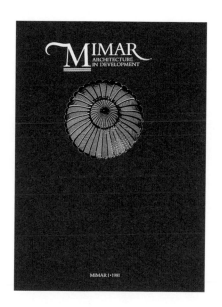

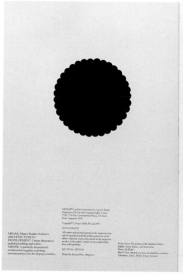

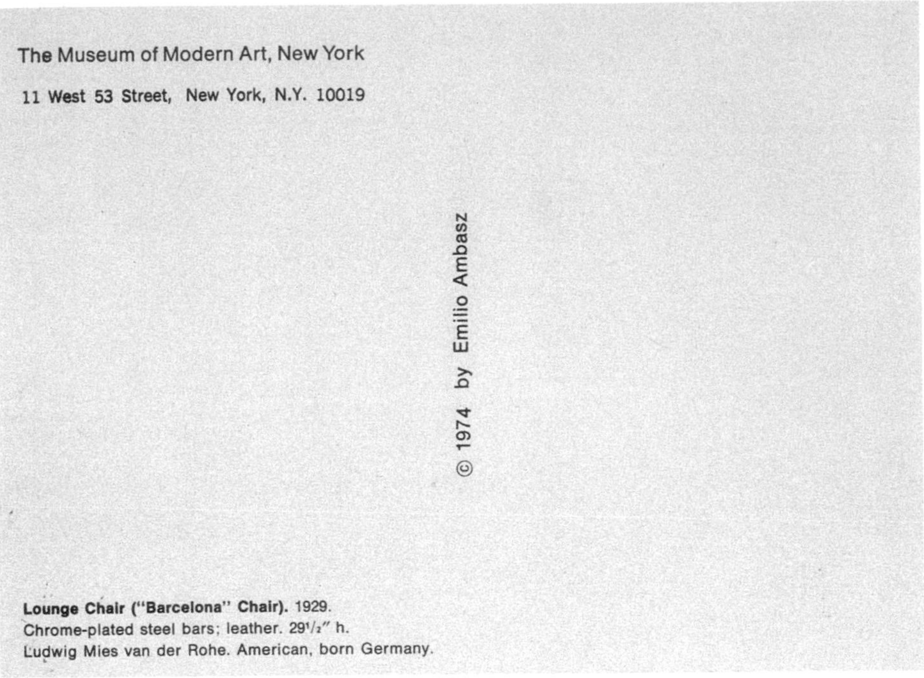

The Museum of Modern Art, New York

11 West 53 Street, New York, N.Y. 10019

© 1974 by Emilio Ambasz

Lounge Chair ("Barcelona" Chair). 1929.
Chrome-plated steel bars; leather. 29$^1/_2$" h.
Ludwig Mies van der Rohe. American, born Germany.

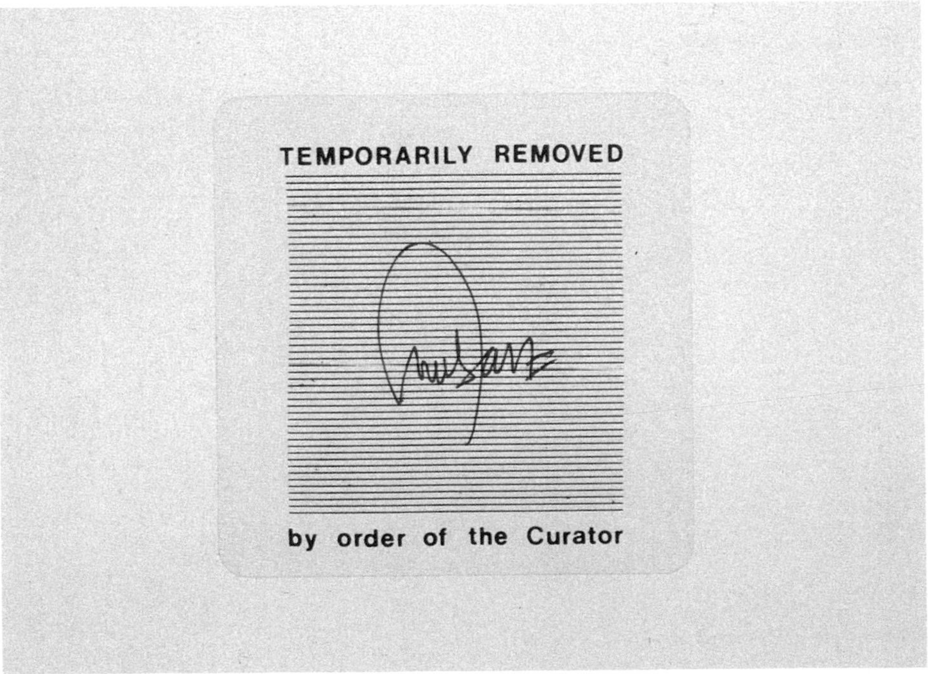

TEMPORARILY REMOVED

by order of the Curator

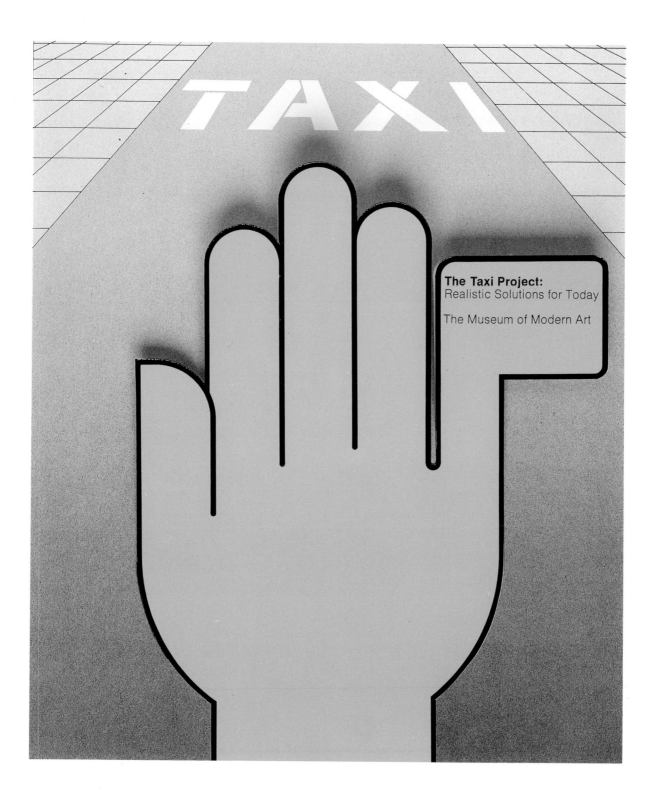

The Taxi Project:
Realistic Solutions for Today

The Museum of Modern Art

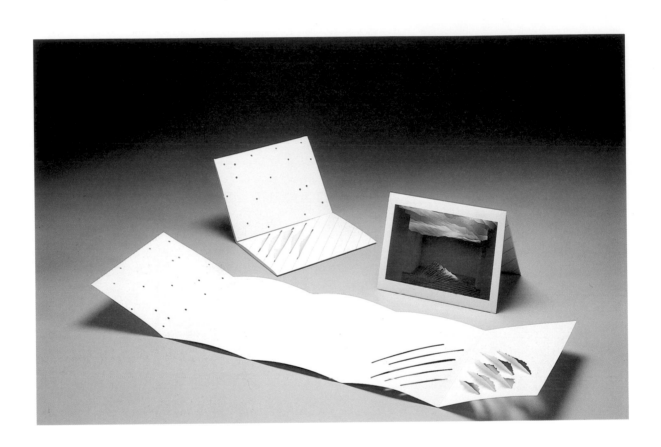

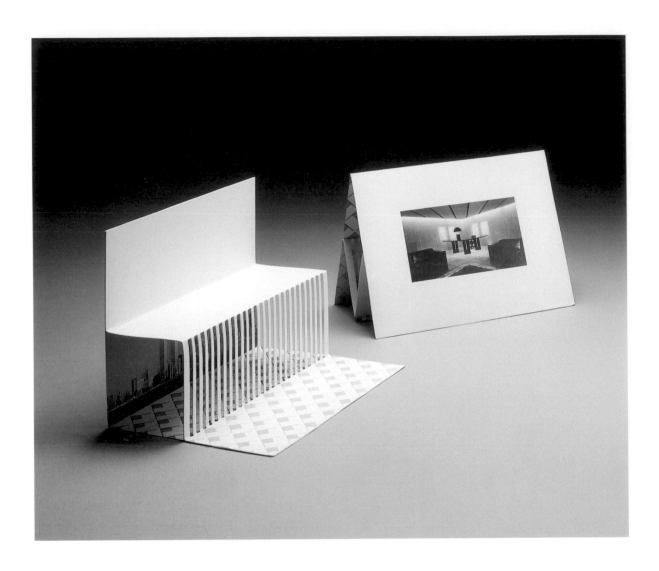

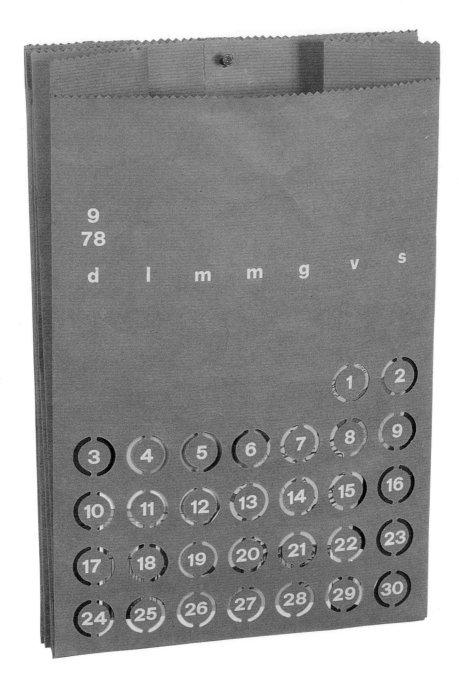

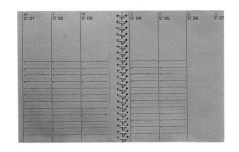

316.

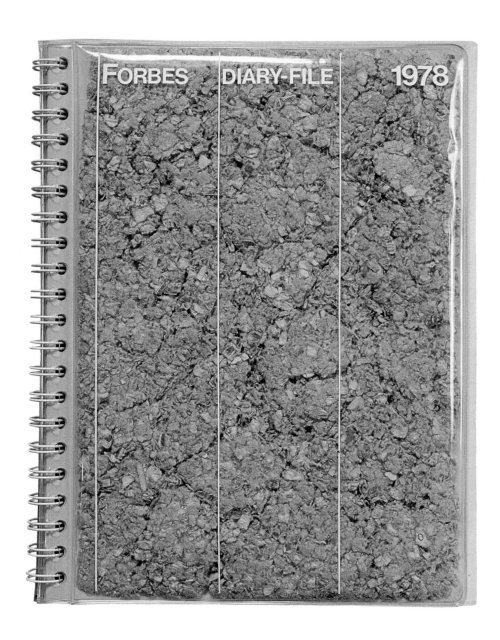

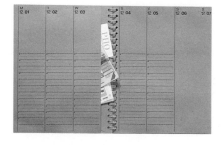

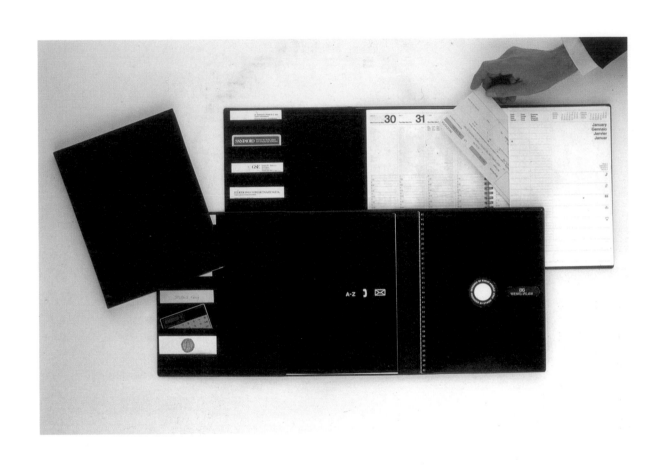

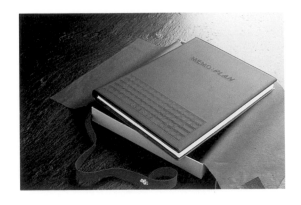

MYCAL GROUP

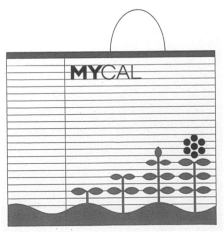

WORLD MAN: BUCKY FULLER POSTER, 1966 (p. 299). This double-layered poster, with the hexagonal cut-out of the front layer and the concentric die-cut rings of the back layer that can be folded and inter-locked to suggest a geodesic dome, evokes the work of its famous subject, Buckminster Fuller.

GEIGY GRAPHICS POSTER, 1966 (pp. 300–301). This poster invites, through its dominant die-cut letter form, the interaction and participation of the viewer. The letter "G" of Geigy is quickly associated with this progressive patron of graphics, and the limitless compositional options suggest the constant possibility of discovery in both the pharmaceutical and design fields.

SURFACE AND ORNAMENT POSTER, 1982 (p. 202). The colors employed and the accordion-like folds of the poster effectively communicate the two primary benefits of this new Formica product, Colorcore: the availability of a subtle palette and the ability, because of the material's homogeneous mass of color, to create concave and/or convex seams without the tell-tale black line that is normally associated with plastic laminates.

AXIS POSTER, 1985 (p. 303). This poster for a show of Ambasz's work adopts the motif of one of his projects and reproduces it through die-cutting, embossing, and the printing of subtle gradations, all of which combine to create a simple and evocative image.

ITALY: THE NEW DOMESTIC LANDSCAPE POSTER, 1972 (p. 304). Designed to advertise the exhibition of the same name, this vitrine poster is composed of thirty-six transparent plexiglass boxes, each of which contains a number of loose die-cut figures representative of the design objects on display. Sealed in their individual containers, each identical set of cut outs presents a unique composition to the viewer, suggesting the infinite variations possible within the new domestic landscape.

ITALY: THE NEW DOMESTIC LANDSCAPE BOOK COVER, 1972 (p. 305). This book cover of folded vellum creates a pocket for the same die-cut elements used in the exhibit poster and allows the elements the freedom to move about and combine randomly. Every time the reader opens the book, or merely moves it, the relationship is altered, suggesting the influence and impact man has over the environments he creates for himself.

MIMAR, 1980 (pp. 306–307). Mimar in Arabic means master builder. This quarterly magazine, created by the Aga Khan to foster an appreciation of Islamic architecture, draws on its subject matter, literally and figuratively, for its cover design. Like Islamic architecture, where the interior of a dwelling is its substance, and the facade by means of grilles and perforations suggests the nature of its interior, each Mimar cover is die-cut to provide a glimpse of the image printed on the first page. The reader provided with this fragment is enticed into "entering" the magazine.

TAXI PROJECT BOOK COVER, 1976 (p. 308). The book cover shows the symbol designed for the exhibition of the same name held at the Museum of Modern Art in New York. The symbol, resembling a hand hailing a taxi, has in this case been die cut so that it can project up at an angle from the book.

BARCELONA CHAIR POSTCARD, 1974 (p. 309). Printed on standard card stock to resemble the Museum of Modern Art's other post cards, this card playfully replaces the image of Mies van der Rohe's Barcelona chair with a stick-on label that reads "Temporarily Removed by Order of Curator" signed by the museum's Design Curator.

RESIDENCE AU LAC CARD, 1983 (p. 310). Produced to celebrate the renovation of an apartment building in Lugano, Switzerland, the die-cut and photographic elements of this card depict the building's lobby, which features a marble floor with vertical slabs that evoke the hills surrounding Lugano's lake, and a ceiling of silk cut-outs suggestive of clouds.

PERSONAL STATIONERY, redesign 1977 (p. 311). A combination of scoring, perforating and die-cutting allows a standard letter size sheet of paper to function simply and elegantly as its own mailing envelope. The die-cut hole allows the folded sheet to be sealed with nothing more than a postage stamp.

BANK BRUXELLES LAMBERT, NEW YORK CARD, 1985 (p. 312). Produced to celebrate the first anniversary of the bank's opening, this card is a quiet reminder of the bank's existence in an over-solicited market. The vertical die-cuts suggest both the security of bank window bars and the curtain of silk fringes that veil the bank's views, both interior and exterior. The photograph, like the trompe l'oeil elements of the bank's interior, calls into question the veracity of representation.

SEEDS GREETING CARD, 1973 (p. 313). Translucent drafting vellum is folded to form a pocket for sunflower seeds that can be planted. Once folded, the pocket serves as its own mailing envelope, and is sealed by means of a postage stamp affixed through a circular die-cut.

CALENDAR MEMORY BAGS, 1970 (pp. 314-315). Both the brown bag and the inter-office envelope version of this calendar provide the opportunity to hold onto whatever one wishes to keep of the past while also planning for the future. In this way, the calendar functions as a physical reminder of the past as it points toward the future.

DIARY FILE AGENDA, 1973 (pp. 316-317). In addition to its use as a normal week-at-a-glance diary, the weekly envelopes are used to file receipts, expense records, tickets, mementos, etc. Each envelope has a tucked-in flap to keep filed elements from falling out. The flap can also be used to seal the envelope's contents. The shredded money in the cover and the seeds in the back suggest a cyclical nature, not just of the calendar but of consumption as well. Having "spent" the year, one closes the book and is offered the promise of renewal: seeds that will produce trees that will be cut down, pulped, and used to print more money.

MEMO-PLAN AGENDA, 1985 (pp. 318-319). The agenda features a series of bound-in envelopes which doubles as files for gathering receipts, records, invoices, etc. With the transformation of the agenda format from a page into an envelope, the agenda adds to its capacity to plan the future and the ability to recall and preserve the past. This feature of remembering the present and planning the future is especially useful when preparing tax returns. This agenda program consists of four models: Week-at-a-Glance, Two weeks-at-a-Glance, Two weeks at a Glance, Pocket agenda, and Daily Agenda.

MYCAL GROUP IDENTITY, 1987 (p. 320). This logotype and symbol, developed for a Japanese company, draws on the eastern tradition of narrative symbols rather than the western tradition of static ones. Suggesting a cyclical progression of the seasons and life, the symbol reflects the company's very real concern with the quality of life of its employees and customers.

CHIOCCIOLA. 1988 (p. 321). This symbol, developed for a client who for years has been identified by the shell of the snail, represents the growth and expansion of the client's company. The shell is normally associated with the dwelling, an appropriate association for a real estate company. Now the snail takes flight, enjoying limitless horizons.

References

EMILIO AMBASZ

Emilio Ambasz, born in 1943 in Argentina, studied at Princeton University. He completed the undergraduate program in one year and earned, the next year, a Master's Degree in Architecture from the same institution. He served as Curator of Design at the Museum of Modern Art in New York (1970–76), where he directed and installed numerous influential exhibits on architecture and industrial design, among them "Italy: The New Domestic Landscape," in 1972; "The Architecture of Luis Barragan," in 1974; and "The Taxi Project," in 1976.

Mr. Ambasz was the two-term President of the Architectural League (1981–85). A co-founder of the Institute for Architecture and Urban Studies in New York, he taught at Princeton University's School of Architecture, was visiting professor at the Hochschule für Gestaltung in Ulm, Germany, and has lectured at many American Universities.

Mr. Ambasz's large number of projects include the Museum of American Folk Art in New York City and the innovative design of the Conservatory at the San Antonio Botanical Center, Texas, recently inaugurated. Among his award-winning projects are the Grand Rapids Art Museum in Michigan, winner of a *1976 Progressive Architecture Award*, a house for a couple in Cordoba, Spain, winner of a *1980 Progressive Architecture Award*, and a *1985 Progressive Architecture* award for the Conservatory at the San Antonio Botanical Center, Texas. His Banque Bruxelles Lambert in Lausanne, Switzerland, a bank interior, received a *1983 Annual Interiors Award* as well as a Special Commendation from the jury. His design for the Banque Bruxelles Lambert branch in Milan, Italy, and his design for their New York City branch at Rockefeller Center have been completed. He won the First Prize and Gold Medal in the closed competition to design the Master Plan for the Universal Exhibition of 1992, which will take place in Seville, Spain, to celebrate the 500th anniversary of America's discovery. This project was also granted a *1986 Architectural Projects Award* from the American Institute of Architects, New York. The headquarters he designed for the Financial Guaranty Insurance Company of New York won the Grand Prize of the *1987 International Interior Design Award* of the United Kingdom, as well as the *1986 IDEA Award* from the Industrial Designers Society of America (IDSA). He won First Prize in the 1986 closed competition for the Urban Plan for the Eschenheimer Tower in Frankfurt, West Germany. The magazine *Progressive Architecture* in 1987 and the American Institute of Architects, New York, in its *1986 Architectural Projects Award*, cited for award the Mercedes Benz Showroom he designed in 1986.

Mr. Ambasz represented America at the 1976 Venice Biennale. He has been the subject of numerous international publications as well as museum and art gallery exhibitions, principal among them the Leo Castelli Gallery, the Corcoran Gallery, the Museum of Modern Art, New York, the Philadelphia Institute of Contemporary Art and the Chicago Art Institute. An exhibition entitled "Emilio Ambasz: 10 Years of Architecture, Graphic and Industrial Design" was held in Milan in the fall of 1983, travelling to Madrid in May '84, and Zurich in the fall of '84. Among others, the international publications *Domus, Space and Design, Architectural Record* and *Architecture plus Urbanism* have dedicated special issues to his architectural work. The Axis Design and Architecture Gallery of Tokyo dedicated a special exhibition of his work in April, 1985. In 1986, the Institute of Contemporary Art of Geneva, Switzerland, at "Halle Sud" and, in 1987, the "Arc-en-Ciel" Gallery of the Centre of Contemporary Art in Bordeaux, France, also presented one-man shows of his work.

Mr. Ambasz also holds a number of industrial and mechanical design patents. He is the Chief Design Consultant for the Cummins Engine Co., a company internationally celebrated for its enlightened support of architecture and design. Mr. Ambasz has received numerous industrial design awards. Included among them are the *Gold Prize* awarded for his co-design of the Vertebra Seating System by the IBD (USA) in 1977, the *SMAU Prize* (Italy) in 1979, and the coveted *Compasso d'Oro* (Italy) in 1981. The Vertebra chair is included in the Design Collections of the Museum of Modern Art, New York, and the Metropolitan Museum of Art, New York. The Museum of Modern Art, New York, has also included in its Design Collection his Flashlight, a design also cited for awards by the *Compasso d'Oro* (Italy) in 1987 and the *IDSA*. His design for Cummins' N14 Diesel Engine won the 1985 *Annual Design Review* from *Industrial Design* magazine. This publication also awarded him similar prizes in 1980 for his Logotec spotlight range (which also received the 1980 *IDSA Design Excellence Award*), in 1983 for the Osiris spotlight range, as well as in 1986 for his design of Escargot, an air filter designed for Fleetguard Incorporated. In 1987 the Industrial Designer's Society of America granted its *Industrial Design Excellence Award Winner* top award for his Soffio, a modular lighting system. In 1988, the IDSA again awarded him the same top honor for AquaColor, a watercolor set. The Tenth Biennial of Industrial Design (BIO 10, Ljubljana, 1984) granted Mr. Ambasz their *Jury Special Award* "for his many contributions to the design field."

Publications by Emilio Ambasz

1988

Mimar 27 (January-March 1988): Cover, and all covers for this quarterly since its founding in 1981.

1987

"Carrelli Elevatori a Wall Street." *l'Arca* Vol. 1. no. 1 (January/February 1987).

"Design Review." *AXIS* Vol. 23 (Spring 1987):p. 105.

"Design Review." *AXIS* Vol. 22 (Winter 1987):p. 105.

"Emilio Ambasz." *Summarios*. Buenos Aires, Argentina: 1987. pp. 8–15.

"Emilio Ambasz: A Decade of Architecture, Industrial and Graphic Design." *Emilio Ambasz* Editor. Tironi, Giordano. Halle Sud, Geneva, Switzerland: Institute of Contemporary Arts (March 1987).

1986

The 1986 Design Zoo. General Editor. Sudjic, Deyan Editor. Ambasz, Emilio. First. New York: John Calmann and King Ltd. and Cross River Press Ltd., 1986.

"Ambasz, Emilio." *Contemporary Landscape from the Horizon of Postmodern Design*. Kyoto/Tokyo, Japan: The National Museum of Modern Art, September 11–October 20, 1985 and December 7, 1985–January 19, 1986.

"Ancient Court Music Beaten Up!" *Space Design no. 8601* 1986: p. 57.

"Chi E Luis Barragan." *Casa Vogue* (June 1986): pp. 94–109.

"La Citta del Design." *Halle Sud Magazine*, 1986. p. 4.

"Design Review." *AXIS* Vol. 21. (Autumn 1986).

"Emilio Ambasz." *Il Giardino d'Europe*. Editor. Vezzosi, Alessandro. Milan: Mazzotta, 1986. pp. 202–204.

"The Italian Influence." *Interior Design in the 20th Century*. Editors. Tate, Allen, and Smith, C. Ray. New York: Harper & Row, 1986.

"Italian Design—A 15-Year Perspective." *AXIS* Vol. 21. (Autumn 1986): p. 50.

"Luis Barragan." *House and Garden* (February 1986): pp. 18–28.

"Spain: Columbus Expo." *TWA Ambassador* (December 1986): p. 9.

with Smith, Philip. "A Millenarian Hope: The Architecture of Emilio Ambasz." *The Harvard Architecture Review*. New York: Rizzoli International Publications, Inc., 1986. pp. 96–103.

1985

"Ambasz, Emilio." *Contemporary Landscape from the Horizon of Postmodern Design* Kyoto/Tokyo, Japan: The National Museum of Modern Art, September 11–October 20, 1985 and December 7, 1985–January 19, 1986.

"Contract and Residential Furniture Logotec Spotlight Range." *Industrial Design Excellence USA*. USA: The Design Foundation, 1980–1985. p. 13.

"Design Review." *AXIS* Vol. 17. (Autumn 1985): pp. 3, 38–41.

"Emilio Ambasz: Botanical Pleasures." *Domus* no. 667 (December 1985): pp. 14–17.

"Exhibition." *The Commercial Architecture* Vol. 30. no. 6 (June 1985): pp. 244–245.

"Exhibition & Lecture Series of Work by Young Architects: Competition Winners." Urban Center Galleries, New York (May 1985).

"Furniture and Furnishings Dorsal Seating Range." *Industrial Design Excellence USA*. USA: The Design Foundation, 1980–1985. p. 44.

"Introduction." *Intercepting Light*. Ando, Tadao. Japan: Designer's Brochure, 1985.

"La libreria nel giardino." *Gran Bazaar* (December/January 1985): p. 140.

"Manoir D'Angoussart." *The Princeton Journal* Vol. 2. 1985. pp. 128–131.

"New Work of Shiro Kuramata." *AXIS* Vol. 16. (Summer 1985): pp. 60–61, 63.

1984

"L'Arte Dans L'Eau: New Orleans Museum of Art." *Domus* no. 651 (June 1984): pp. 30–31.

"Dar Forma Póetica a lo Pragmático: Notas Sobre Mi Obra de Diseño." *Diario 16* (May 11, 1984): p. 5 (Hogar 16).

Emilio Ambasz. Italy: Grafis Editions, 1984.

"Emilio Ambasz: The Innovator for Aiming at Utopia." *Idea: International Advertising Art* Vol. 32. no. 187 (November 1984): pp. 88–95.

"Fabula Rasa." *Via 7: The Building of Architecture*. Cambridge and London: The MIT Press, 1984. p. 87.

"La Folly de Emilio: El Hombre es una isla." *Follies: MOPU Arquitectura* (May/June 1984): pp. 34–37.

"Houston Center Plaza." *Architectural Design—Urbanism* (January/February 1984): pp. 46–47.

"Il Caffè della Città." *Domus* (April 1984): p. 116.

"Notas acerca de mi labor de diseño." *Diseño* (May 1984): pp. 71–75.

"Obras y Proyectos, 1972–1984: Entre la Arcadia y la Utopia." *Colegio Oficial de Arquitectos de Madrid*, 1984.

"La Piazza Interminabile: Il Caffè della Città." *Domus* no. 649 (April 1984): pp. 14–19, 116.

"Plaza Major, Salamanca." *Architectural Design—Urbanism* (January/February 1984): pp. 44–45.

"Popular Pantheon." *The Architectural Review* no. 1054 (December 1984): p. 35.

"Three Projects by Enzo Mari . . ." *Domus* no. 649 (April 1984): pp. 14–19.

1983

"Automatisch-Dynamisches Sitzen." *MD Moebel Interior Design* (October 10, 1983): pp. 56–57.

Dal Cucchiaio alla Cittá: Nell'itinerario di 100 Designers. Venosta, Carla. Milan: Electa, 1983. pp. 26–27.

"The Dorsal Seating Range." *Innovation*. McLean, VA: Industrial Designers Society of America (Winter 1983): Vol. 2: pp. 23–25.

"Emilio Ambasz: Dieci anni di Architettura, Grafica, Design in un Multivision Ralizzato de Domus." *Centrodomus* (October 24, 1983).

"Emilio's Folly: Man is an Island." *Follies: Architecture for the Late-Twentieth Century Landscape*. Editor. Archer, B.J. New York: Rizzoli, 1983. pp. 34–37.

"Houston Center Plaza, Houston." *Lotus International*. 39. Venice, Italy: Gruppo Electa S.p.A., (March 1983): pp. 65–69.

"Italy: The New Domestic Landscape Exhibit, MOMA 1972." *Domus*, 1983. p. 27.

"La Mostra 'Italy: The New Domestic Landscape' presentata . . . ebbe un forte e profondo impatto." *Domus*, 1983.

"Premios Kones 1982-Artes Visuales." *Diploma al Merito: Libro de Oro de las Artes Visuales Argentinas*. Buenos Aires, Argentina: La Fundacion Konex, 1983. p. 86.

"Review of Herbert Muschamp's." *Man About Town*. Muschamp, Herbert. Cambridge, Massachusetts: MIT Press, 1983.

"Salamanca: The Plaza Mayor." *Lotus International*. 39. Venice, Italy: Gruppo Electra S.p.A., March 1983. pp. 62–64.

"Skin and Bones." Milan, Italy: Electa Alcantara, 1983. p. 20.

"Visual Monologue." *Ivan Chermayeff*. Vienna: Collages, Galerie Ulysses, 1983.

with Jakobson, Barbara. "La Casa Bifronte/Janus's House." *Domus* no. 635 (January 1983): pp. 34–39.

1982

"Ambasz': Los que Conozco Diseñan los Domingos." *Vivienda* no. 235 (February 1982): p. 8.

"Beyond Metaphor, Beyond Form." *Meanings of Modernism: Design Quarterly* no. 118–119, 1982. pp. 4–11.

"La Citta del Design." *Skyline* (November 1982): p. 24.

Il Design Oggi in Italia Tra Produzione, Consumo E Qualcos' Altro. Ambasz, Emilio. Italy: Museo Villa Pignatelli. (June 1982): p. 27.

"Milano, 1920–1940." *Skyline* (November 1982): pp. 18–19.

"P/A Second Annual Conceptual Furniture Competition." *Progressive Architecture* Vol. LXIII. no. 5 (May 1982): pp. 158–169.

"Preface." *Precursors of Post-Modernism*. New York: The Architectural League, 1982.

"Reportaje: Emilio Ambasz." *Summa* no. 174 (May 1982): pp. 21–22.

"Wait Until You See the Next Olivetti Machine." *Memphis 82*. Milan: Stampa Nava Milano S.p.A., 1982. p. 4.

1981

"Columbus il Mito." *La Mia Casa* no. 141 (October 1981): pp. 106–107.

"Farewell, Caro Maestro." *Progressive Architecture* Vol. LXII. no. 5 (May 1981): p. 117.

"P/A First Annual Conceptual Furniture Competition." *Progressive Architecture* Vol. LXII. no. 11 (May 1981): pp. 150–155.

"Post Modernism, the Social Aspect." *Performing Arts* Vol. 5. no. 3, 1981. pp. 59–60.

"La Proposta di Ambasz." *Domus* no. 622 (November 1981): p. 49.

"The Return of Marco Polo." *Design: Vignelli*. New York: Rizzoli International Publications, 1981.

with Meritet, Michael. "The Four Gates to Columbus." *Artists and Architects Collaboration*. Editor. Diamonstein, Barbaralee. New York: Whitney Library of Design, 1981. p. 130–135.

1980

"Ambasz." *Domus* no. 610 (October 1980): p. 20.

"Contract and Residential Furniture: Logotec Spotlight Range." *Industrial Design Excellence USA*. USA: The Design Foundation, 1980–1985. p. 13.

"A Cooperative of Mexican-American Grape Growers, California, 1976." *Design Quarterly* Vol. 113/114, 1980. pp. 26–27.

"Furniture and Furnishings: Dorsal Seating Range." *Industrial Design Excellence USA*. USA: The Design Foundation, 1980–1985. p. 44.

"Imponderable Substance." *Progressive Architecture* Vol. LXI. no. 9 (September 1980): pp. 138–141.

"Notes About My Design Work." *Architecture and Urbanism* Vol. 80. no. 5 (May 1980): pp. 33–60.

"Projet D'une Maison Pour un Couple, A Cordoba, Espagne." *Techniques et Architecture* no. 331 (June/July 1980): pp. 118–119.

"Working Fables: A Collection of Design Tales for Skeptic Children." *Architecture and Urbanism* (May 1980): pp. 107–114.

1979

"Deux Propositions Alternatives." *Techniques et Architecture* no. 325 (June/July 1979): pp. 101–104.

"Favolette di Progettazione (Working Fables)." *Modo* (September/October 1979): p. 56.

"Luis Barragan." *Global Architecture 48* 1979.

1978

"Architecture is the Reply to Man's Passion and Hunger." *The AIA Journal* (Mid-May 1978): p. 231.

"Emilio Ambasz." *Global Eye '78 7 New Design Powers*. Kamekura, Yusaku. Japan: Japan Design Committee, March 3–8, 1978.

Foreword, *High Tech: The Industrial Style and Source Book for the Home*. Kron, Joan, and Slesin, Suzanne. New York Clarkson N. Potter, Inc. Publishers, 1978.

"Views Credit: Chair Development." *Progressive Architecture* Vol. LIX. no. 2 (December 1978): p. 8.

1977

Designer. *Architecture 1*. Organizer. Apraxine, Pierre. New York: Leo Castelli Gallery, October 22–November 1 1977.

"Centro Mexicano de Cálculo Aplicado SA." *Summarios* n 11 (September 1977): p. 17.

"Centros Comunitarios Educacionales y Agrarios." *Summarios* no. 11 (September 1977): pp. 18–19.

"Community Art Center." *Summarios* no. 11 (Septemb 1977): p. 28.

"Conjunto de Viviendas en un Establecimiento Agricola *Summarios* no. 11 (September 1977): pp. 26–27.

"Cooperativa de Viñateros Mexicano-Norteamericanos *Summarios* no. 11 (September 1977): pp. 20–22.

"Le Designer Comme Realisateur." *l'Architecture d'A jourd'hui* Vol. 193. (October 1977): pp. 64–66.

"Emilio Ambasz." *A View of Contemporary World Architec* Vol. 52. no. 14 (December 1977): pp. 186–187.

"For Sale: Advanced Design, Tested and Ready to Run." *D sign* no. 346 (October 1977): pp. 50–53.

"Moral: Una Condición de Prediseño." *Summarios* no. (September 1977): p. 16.

"Una Declaración Sobre mi Obra." *Summarios* no. 11 (S tember 1977): pp. 15.

"La Univerciudad (Borrador)." *Summarios* no. 11 (Septem 1977): p. 17.

"Working Fables Sleepwalker's Dream." *Modo* no. 3 (Septe ber/October 1977): p. 56.

1976

The Architecture of Luis Barragan. New York: The Muse of Modern Art, 1976.

"Commentary: Emilio Ambasz." *Princeton's Beaux Arts Its New Academicism*. Editor. Wurmfeld, Michael. N York: The Institute for Architecture and Urban Stud 1976. p. 25.

"Special Feature: Up-and-Coming Light: Emilio Ambas His Works and Thoughts: A Statement About my Wo *Space Design* (October 1976): pp. 4–44.

The Taxi Project: Realistic Solutions for Today. Editor. basz, Emilio. New York: The Museum of Modern Art, J 17–September 6, 1976.

1975

"Anthology for a Spatial Buenos Aires." *Casabella* no. (February 1975): pp. 6–7.

"Coda: A Pre-Design Condition: A Selection from 'Work Fables'—A Collection of Design Tales for Skeptic C dren." *Casabella* no. 401 (May 1975): pp. 4–5.

"Manhattan, Capital of the 20th Century. A Selection f 'Working Fables'—A Collection of Schematic De Tales for Skeptic Children." *Casabella* no. 397 (Jan 1975): p. 4.

"The Univercity: A Selection from 'Working Fables'—A lection of Design Tales for Skeptic Children." *Casab* no. 399 (March 1975): pp. 8–9.

Walter Pichler: Projects. Editor. Ambasz, Emilio. New Y Museum of Modern Art, September 12–October 28, 1

1974

"La Città del Disegno: A Selection from 'Working Fables Collection of Design Tales for Skeptic Children." *C bella* no. 394 (October 1974): pp. 4–5.

"Design im Zeitalter der Aufklärung." *Form* no. 68 (M 1974): pp. 32–33.

"The Enlightened Client: A Selection from 'Working bles'—A Collection of Design Tales for Skeptic Child *Casabella* no. 396 (December 1974): pp. 4–5.

"A Selection from Working Fables: A Collection of De Tales for Skeptic Children." *Oppositions 4* (Oct 1974): pp. 65–74.

1972

Italy: The New Domestic Landscape. Editor. Ambasz, lio. New York: Museum of Modern Art, May 26–Sep ber 11, 1972.

1971

"Instituciones y Artefactos para una Sociedad Postecno gica." *Summa* no. 37 (May 1971): pp. 30–36.

1969

"The Formulation of a Design Discourse." *Perspecta* n (1969): pp. 57–71.

Publications on Emilio Ambasz

1988

"Emilio Ambasz San Antonio Botanical Conservatory, Texas." *Architectural Design* Vol. 58. no. 3/4 (April 1988): pp. 46–47.

Wrede, Stuart. "Geigy Graphics." *The Modern Poster*. New York: The Museum of Modern Art, 1988. p. 198.

1987

Aldersey-Williams, Hugh. "Widening Horizons." *TWA Ambassador* (June 1987): p. 68.

Barna, Joel Warren. "Light and Fog in San Antonio." *Texas Architect* Vol. 37. no. 4 (July/August 1987): pp. 28–31.

Buchanan, Peter. "Curtains for Ambasz." *The Architectural Review* no. 1083 (May 1987): pp. 73–77.

"Designing with a lot of Bottle." *Design* no. 460 (April 1987): p. 46.

"Emilio Ambasz: Una Mostra di Progetti." *Domus* no. 683 (May 1987): pp. 10–11.

Goldberger, Paul. "A Spacious Sunken Garden will Bloom in San Antonio." *The New York Times*. June 11, 1987, pp. C1 and C10.

Goodrich, Kristina. "Profiles of the 1986 Industrial Design Excellence Award Winners." *Innovations* (Winter 1987): pp. 7–9.

Imatake, Midori. "Brilliant Talent—Emilio Ambasz: So Much is Expected of him in the Future." *Idea* no. 202, 1987. pp. 66–73.

Léon, Hilde, and Wohlhage, Konrad. "Fragment, Leerraum, Geschwindigkeit und das Bild der klassischen Stadt." *Bauwelt 36 Stadtbauwelt 95* (September 1987): p. 1335.

Listings for San Antonio Events." *Texas Monthly* Vol. 15. no. 6 (June 1987): p. 70.

Mercedes Benz Showroom." *Progressive Architecture* Vol. LXVIII. no. 1 (January 1987): pp. 104–105.

Murphy, Jim et al. "34th Annual P/A Awards." *Progressive Architecture* (January 1987): pp. 104–105.

New Products and Literature." *Progressive Architecture* (March 1987): p. 169.

News Briefs." *Architectural Record* (April 1987): p. 47.

xposicion Universal Expo '92 Sevilla: Ideas para una ordenacion del recinto. Editor. Ruiz, Manuel Olivencia. Seville: Comisario General Exposicion Universal Sevilla 1992, 1987. pp. 9–24.

mith, C. Ray et al. "1986 Architectural Projects Awards: What Might Be." *Oculus An Eye on New York Architecture* Vol. 48. no. 6 (February 1987): pp. 4 and 15.

nterior Design in 20th Century America: A History. Smith, C. Ray. New York: Harper & Row, 1987. pp. 301–303 and 312.

ickle, Katherine. "IIDA International Interior Design Award 1987." *Interior Design* (April 1987): pp. 35–39.

ironi, Giordano. "La Citta del Design; Entre l'Objet et la Ville; Entretien avec Emilio Ambasz." *Halle Sud Geneve* no. 13 (January/February/March 1987).

ruppin, Andrea. "Inventive Genius." *Interiors* (April 1987): pp. 171–187.

andeuvre, Elianede. "Design/France." *Fusion Planning* no. 13 (July 1987): pp. 78–81.

aisman, Marina. "Emilio Ambasz." *Summarios* (January 1987): pp. 8–15.

estweek 87 Program and Products." *Designers West* Special Edition. (March 1987).

86

76–1986 Orgatechnik." *MD* (October 1986): pp. 44–46.

serga, Fiorella. "Scultura di Lastre: Un Capolavoro di Emilio Ambasz." *Marmo Macchine* no. 68 (Bimestre 2, 1986): pp. 118–120.

ventieth Century Style and Design. Bayley, Stephen; Garner, Philippe; Sudjic, Deyan. New York: Van Nostrand Reinhold Company, 1986. pp. 260–261, 292, 298.

enner, Douglas. "Magic Mountains." *Architectural Record* (June 1986): pp. 132–135.

chanan, Peter. "Spanish Isles." *The Architects' Journal* (September 24, 1986): pp. 32–33.

eer dans le Cree. Directors. Burkhardt, F., and Boiret, Y. Paris: Electa France, May 28–September 7, 1986. pp. 178–179.

rd and Image: Posters from the Collection of the Museum of Modern Art. Editor. Constantine, Mildred. New York: The Museum of Modern Art, 1986. p. 136.

llon, David. "Moonscape in the Sun." *Spirit* (April 1986): pp. 68–119.

ler, Martin. "L System." *Surface and Ornament*. Curator. Rogers-Lafferty, Sarah. Cincinnati, Ohio: The Contemporary Arts Center, 1986.

ovannini, Joseph. "Offices move Boldly Backward or Playfully Forward." *The New York Times*. (January 19, 1986): p. F8.

nna, Annetta. " 'Equipment' Escargot Air Filter." *ID Magazine* Vol. 33. no. 4 (July/August 1986): p. 79.

roduction." *Emerging Voices*. Editor. Allen, Gerald. New York: The Architectural League of New York, 1986. p. 6.

amus, Julith. "Chairs that Ease the Spine." *Newsweek* Vol. CVII. no. 24 (June 16, 1986): p. 3.

ez Palanco, Rafael, and Marin, Luis. "Siviglia 1992 . . . Un Concorso di idee per l'Esposizione Universale." *Domus* (October 1986): pp. 18–29.

Modern Redux: Critical Alternatives for Architecture in the Next Decade. New York: Grey Art Gallery and Study Center, New York University, 1986.

Morton, David. "Perspectives: Milan Furniture Fair." *Progressive Architecture* (December 1986): pp. 38–40.

Pearlman, Chee. "Environments." *ID Magazine of International Design Annual Design Review 1986*. USA: Design Publications, Inc., July/August 1986. Vol. 33: p. 62.

"Plaza Mayor, Salamanca, Spain." *architektur + wettbewerbe* no. 127 (September 1986): p. 21.

Reif, Rita. "Rare Glimpse of the Furniture of a Modern Dutch Master." *The New York Times* (July 13, 1986): p. 30H.

Rinaldi, Paolo. "A Lugano Marmo e Nuvole." *Casa Vogue* no. 172 (March 1986): pp. 170–171.

L'eau en Formes. La Societe Generale des Eaux Minerales de Vittel. Centre Georges Pompidou, November 1986.

"Spain: Columbus Expo." *TWA Ambassador* (December 1986): p. 9.

Stewart, Doug. "Modern Designers Still Can't Make the Perfect Chair." *Smithsonian* (April 1986): p. 102.

Tebaldi, Mirko. "Siviglia: Concorso di idee per l'Esposizione Universale 1992." *Domus* no. 677 (November 1986): pp. 80–88.

"The Technology of Horology." *Architectural Record* (January 1986): p. 57.

"Time Piece." *AXIS* Vol. 18. (Winter 1986): p. 74.

Vider, Elise. "Light." *Almanac* (September/October 1986): pp. 38–42.

Yerkes, Susan. "Design for the Times." *The Continental* (February 1986): pp. 29–33.

1985

"21 Progettisti alla Ricerca delle Proprie Affinita." *Arredorama* no. 144 (March 1985): pp. 30–32.

Abdulac, Samir. "Tokyo: Argentinian Designers' Show." *Mimar* no. 16 (April/June 1985): p. 16.

"Le Affinita Elettive." *Domus* no. 660 (April 1985): pp. 81–88.

"Le Affinita Elettive di Ventuno Progettisti." *L'Industria del Mobile*. no. 288 (May 1985): pp. 49–58.

"Le Affinita' Elettive." *AXIS* Vol. 15 (Spring 1985): p. 65.

"Agamennone." *Ottagono* no. 76 (March 1985): p. 119.

"Architekt + Designer + Grafiker." *M-D Magazine* (June 1985): pp. 38–41.

"Axis." *AXIS* Vol. 16 (Summer 1985): p. 90.

"Axis Exhibit." *Interior Design News* (June 1985): p. 44.

Ensayos y Apuntos para un Bosquejo Critico Luis Barragan. Barragan, Luis, and Ferrera, Raul. Mexico: Museo Rufino Tamayo, 1985. pp. 23–25.

The Conran Directory of Design. Editor. Bayley, Stephen. New York: Villard Books, 1985. p. 73.

Bernard, April. "Fringe Benefits." *Manhattan, Inc.* (July 1985): pp. 122–123.

Brown, Theodore. "Landscape Strategies: The New Orleans Museum of Art Addition." *The Princeton Journal* Vol. 2. (1985): pp. 186–187.

Brozen, Kenneth. "Working it Out." *Interiors* (September 1985): pp. 190–199 and 222.

Conroy, Sarah Booth. "Toward the Grand Design." *The Washington Post*. (August 24, 1985): pp. 1–9.

"Cordoba House." *AXIS* vol. 15. (September 1985): p. 90.

Corning, Blair. "Conservatory to be 'Unique in S.A.'." *Express-News*. (August 28, 1985): p. 3B.

Diamonstein, Barbara Lee. "Emilio Ambasz." *American Architecture Now II*. New York: Rizzoli, 1985. pp. 19–27.

Dietsch, Deborah K. "Fringe Benefits." *Architectural Record* no. 11 (November 1985): pp. 126–131.

"Elective Affinities." *Arredorama* Vol. 44. (March 1985): pp. 30–32.

"Elective Affinities." *AXIS* Vol. 15. (September 1985): p. 65.

"Emilio Ambasz, Plaza Mayor Salamanca." *Domus* no. 660 (April 1985): pp. 12–13.

"Equipment ID. 1985 Annual Design Review." *Industrial Design* (July/August 1985): p. 107.

Fawcett, Shirley. "Lighting: Out of the Shadows." *Design* no. 439 (July 1985): pp. 32–33.

Fiorentino, Laura. "Botanical Center Planting New Facility." *San Antonio Light* (August 28, 1985): p. C1.

Fonio, DiGiorgio. "The Elective Affinities." *La Mia Casa* no. 178, 1985 pp. 68–71.

Giovannini, Joseph. "Designer's Role, Here vs. Abroad." *The New York Times* (November 14, 1985): pp. 23 and 25.

Giovannini, Joseph. "Made in America: U.S. Product Design." *The New York Times*. (November 14, 1985): pp. C1 & C8.

Greenberg, Mike. "Ambasz Designs Surreal Landscape for San Antonio." *Texas Architect* Vol. 35. no. 2 (March/April 1985): pp. 24–25.

Hanna, Annetta. "Psychodrama in Milan." *Industrial Design* (May/June 1985): pp. 16–21, 74 and 76.

Hendricks, David. "This Architect's Priority: Enhancing Creativity." *Express-News* (June 16, 1985): pp. 1K and 9K.

Huidobro, Michele. "Les Bureaus D'une Banque a New York." *Techniques et Architecture* no. 362 (October/November 1985): pp. 179–180.

"ICISD '85 Interview." *AXIS* Vol. 17. (Autumn 1985): pp. 38–41.

Omnibook 2: Italian Industrial Designers. Editors. Iliprandi, Giancarlo, and Molinari, Pierluigi. Italy: Magnus Edizioni, 1985. p. 20.

Industrial Design Magazine [ID] Annual Design Review. New York: Gallery 91, (October 1985).

"Interior Design News." *Interior Design* (June 1985): p. 44.

"The Lucile Halsell Conservatory: Architectural Design Citation." *Progressive Architecture* (January 1985): pp. 120–121.

Modo (January/February 1985): cover page.

"New & Notable." *Industrial Design* (January/February 1985): p. 76.

Pedretti, Bruno. "Mostre Alla Triennale: Le Affinità Elettive." *Interni* no. 349 (April 1985): pp. 44–53.

Shashaty, Andre. "Modern Industry—A Private Moveable Office Module." *Dun's Business Month* (June 1985): p. 85.

Shaw, Edward. "Argentine Architects Reshape Skylines and U.S." *Argentine News* (August 7, 1985): pp. 40–43.

Smetana, Donatella. "Che Cosa Stanno Facendo." *Casa Vogue* no. 164 (June 1985): p. 221.

Stadt Frankfurt Am Main. 1985. pp. 12–15.

Staebler, Wendy. "Something About a Wall." *Interiors* (September 1985): pp. 200–206.

"Surface & Ornament." The Metropolitan Museum of Art with Formica Corporation and Architecture Club of Miami, (May 1, 1985).

Tapley, Charles. "Buildings & the Land: An Introduction." *Texas Architect* Vol. 35. no. 2 (April 1985): p. 43.

"Things Seen." *Design* no. 439 (July 1985): p. 25.

"Vertebra." *AXIS* Vol. 15. (September 1985): p. 90.

"Vintage Year for Design." *Press Release by ID Magazine* (August 1985).

XIII Biennale de Paris. Paris, France: Grande Halle du Parc de la Villette (March 21, 1985).

1984

"The Alternative Museum." *Tit for Tat Lin*. Curator, Berg, Peter. New York: November 14–December 8, 1984. pp. 6, 11–12 and 23.

"Ambassador to the Interior." *Building Design Journal* (May 1984).

"Arquitectura y Diseño." *Guia del Ocio*. Madrid, Spain (May 1984).

"The Arts Community: Squaring Art with History: Cubism & Constructs." *New York Daily News*. (November 8, 1984).

"Biennial of Industrial Design." *BIO 10 Catalogue*. Yugoslavia: Yugoslavia Biennial (October 1984): pp. 31, 78, 81, 189 and 197.

Brenner, Douglas. "Et in Arcadia Ambasz: Five Projects by Emilio Ambasz & Associates." *Architectural Record* Vol. 172. no. 10 (September 1984): pp. 120–133.

Le Empire du Bureu 1900–2000. Editor. Brisebarre, Jean Jacques. Paris: February 1984. pp. 80 and 210.

Buchanan, Peter. "The Poet's Garden." *The Architectural Review* (June 1984): pp. 50–55.

Buenos Aires a Través de sus Escritore, Artistas y Arquitectos. Curators. Kleihues, Josef P., and Glusberg, Jorge. Buenos Aires, Argentina (October 1984).

Busch, Akiko. "Product Design." *Industrial Design Magazine* (1984): pp. 85, 105 and 141.

Product Design. Editors. Busch, Akiko, et al. New York: Robert Silver & Associates (US Distributors), 1984. pp. 85, 89, 105 and 141.

Mobili come Architettura: Il Disegno della Produzione Zanotta. Casciani, Stefano. Milano: Arcadia Srl, 1984. pp. 105, 110 and 126.

"Cultura y Ocio: Arquitectura y Diseño: Exposicion Emilio Ambasz 1984." *Casa Viva* (May 1984): pp. 64–68.

"Designing a Plaza for Houston." *Lotus International* no. 39 (1984): pp. 62–69.

Dunlap, Davis W. "Future Metropolis." *Omni* (October 1984): pp. 116–123.

Emilio Ambasz 1984: Arquitectura, Diseño Grafico e Industrial. Madrid: MAD Centro de diseño and Galeria Ynguanzo, May 1984.

"Emilio Ambasz: Recent Project." *AMC* no. 6 (December 1984): pp. 4–13.

"Exposición: Emilio Ambasz 1984." *Casa & Jardin* no. 108 (May 1984).

"Exposiciones del Arquitecto Argentino Emilio Ambasz." *Cultura* (May 14, 1984): p. 21.

"Exposión en Madrid: Emilio Ambasz, Creador de Objetos." *Diario 16* (May 4, 1984).

"Floating Architecture in New Orleans." *Design* no. 426 (June 1984): p. 21.

Gaibis, Cecilia. "Cultura: Exposiciones del Arquitecto Argentino Emilio Ambasz: Considerado uno de los Mejores del Mundo." *ABC* (May 14, 1984).

Gandee, Charles. "Offices for Banque Bruxelles Lambert, New York City." *Record Interiors 1984* (Mid-September 1984): pp. 92–97.

Giovanni, Odoni. "L'Arcipelago delle Arti." *Casa Vogue* no. 152 (May 1984): p. 226.

Glancey, Jonathan. "The Gordon Russell Furniture Award." *The Architectural Review* vol. 176. no. 1053 (November 1984): pp. 25–41.

Glueck, Grace. "Tit for Tat Lin." *The New York Times* (November 16, 1984).

Glusberg, Jorge, Curator. "Emilio Ambasz." *Architecture in Latin America Horizonte '82–IBA 84.* Berlin: Internationale Bauausstellung 1984. p. 37.

Concepts of Urban Design. Gosling, David, and Maitland, Barry. New York: St. Martin's Press, 1984. pp. 121–123, 131.

Graff, Vera. "Monumente der Verschwendung." *Du, Die Zeitschrift für Kunst and Kultur* (April 1984): pp. 30–35.

Greer, Norma Richter. "Light as a Tool of Design." *Architecture* (October 1984): p. 55.

Irace, Fulvio. "Piazza A Houston: Un Progetto di Emilio Ambasz." *Diagonalle* (March 1984): pp. 42–43.

"The Island: The Project of Emilio Ambasz for the New Orleans Museum of Art." *Gran Bazar* (June/July 1984): pp. 64–66.

Ito, Kobun. "New Orleans Museum of Art." *Space Design* Vol. 6. no. 237 (June 1984): pp. 49–54.

"Japanese Architecture." *Nikkei Architecture* (December 31, 1984): pp. 34–39.

Kassler, Elizabeth B. "Cordoba House." *Modern Gardens and the Landscape.* New York: The Museum of Modern Art, 1984. p. 130.

Lucan, Jacques. "Emilio Ambasz: Projets Récents." *AMC: Revue D'Architecture* (Decmeber 1984): pp. 4–15.

"MAD." *D.M.A. Hogares* no. 196 (June 1984).

Millán, Liliana. "E Makes Architecture, A Designs Architecture." *La Nación.* July 1, 1984, pp. 2–3.

Millán, Liliana. "Emilio más Ambasz." *La Nación.* July 4, 1984.

Onetti, Jorge. "El Diseño como una de las Bellas Artes." *Diario 16* (May 11, 1984): pp. 4–5 (Hoger 16).

Perales, Marisa. "Ambasz en Madrid." *Arquitectos* no. 77 (April 1984): pp. 38–48.

Samaniego, Fernando. "Los Diseños de Emilio Ambasz." *El Pais* (May 5, 1984).

Santobeña, Andrea. "Un Genial Creador de 'Objetos': Emilio Ambasz: Da Forma Poetica a lo Pragmatico." *El Europeo* (May 31, 1984): pp. 73–74.

"Servicio de Novedades." *Summa* no. 203 (August 1984): p. 81.

"Su Diseño." *Mercado* (May 25, 1984).

Sun, Marjorie, and Hart, Claudia. "Color as Substance: Plastic Laminates." *Industrial Design Magazine* (January/February 1984): pp. 54–57.

Szenasey, Susan S. "Merchant Bankers/At Home Study." *The Office Book Design Series Private and Executive Office.* Editor. Szenasy, Susan S. New York: Facts on File, Inc., 1984. pp. 32–34, 84–85.

"Tendenze & Novità." *Capital Casa* no. 10 (October 1984): pp. 16–17.

Tit for Tat Lin. New York: The Alternative Museum, 1984. pp. 6, 11–12 and 23.

1983

"L'Analisi Economica del Design: Ambasz-Piretti." *E'Design.* October 10–November 7, 1983.

Follies: Architecture for the Late-Twentieth Century Landscape. Archer, B.J. New York: Rizzoli, 1983. pp. 34–37.

"Automatisch-Dynamisches Sitzen." *Moebel Interior Design* (October 10, 1983): pp. 56–57.

Becarra, Blanca. "Dialogo: Con el Arquitecto Emilio Ambasz." *Trama* (May 1983): pp. 20–27.

Boissiére, Olivier. "Di Faccia e di Taglio." *La Mia Casa* (December 1983): p. 100.

Boles, Daralice Donkervoet. "Financial Institution Winner." *Interiors* Vol. CXLII. no. 6 (January 1983): pp. 100–103.

Botta, Mario. "Houston Commentary." *Domus* (May 1983): pp. 2–5.

Brion, Georgia Carrari. "Architettura da Protagonisti con case e Oggetti in Piacevole Misura d'uomo." *La Republica* (October 8, 1983).

Buchanan, Peter. "An Awe-Filled Arcadia: The Architectural Quest of Emilio Ambasz." *Architecture and Urbanism* no. 155 (August 1983): pp. 30–35.

Buchanan, Peter. "High Tech: Another British Thoroughbred." *The Architectural Review* (July 1983): p. 19.

Burgasser, Joan. "1982 Awards Program Profiles: The Dorsal Seating Range—Emilio Ambasz, IDSA and Giancarlo Piretti." *Innovation* Vol. 2. no. 1 (Winter 1983): pp. 23–25.

Busch, Akiko. "Annual Design Review—Contract and Residential." *Industrial Design Magazine* (September/October 1983): pp. 42–44, 49.

Busch, Akiko. "Contract and Residential Furniture." *Product Design* (1982–1983): pp. 105 and 141.

Busch, Akiko. "Home Electronics and Entertainment." *Product Design* (1982–1983): p. 85.

Busch, Akiko. "Who's Who: Award Winning Designers." *Interiors* (January 1983): pp. 120–121.

"Correspondencias: Escultura y Arquitectura en el Museo de Bellas Artes de Bilbao." *El Correo Español* (March 15, 1983): p. 9.

Davis, Douglas. "Arquitectos de Vanguardia Reviven las Construcciones Extravagantes para Jardines." *La Nación.* November 27, 1983.

Davis, Douglas. "Bringing Back the Follies." *Newsweek* (November 14, 1983): p. 104.

de Gorbea, Xabier Saenz. "Correspondencias: 5 Arquitectos—5 Escultores." *DEIA* (March 15, 1983).

Dinelli, Fiamma. "Nuova Sede della Banca Bruxelles Lambert a Losanna/Renovation of a Bank in Lausanne." *L'Industria delle Construzione* no. 140 (June 1983): pp. 54–57.

"Diseno: Emilio Ambasz." *Libro de Oro de Las Artes Visuales Argentinas.* Editor. Ovsejevich, Dr. Luis. Buenos Aires: Fundacion Konex, 1983. p. 86.

"Emilio Ambasz's design Nuove Frontiere e Strategie del Design Italiano degli Anni Ottanta." *It's Design: New frontiers and Strategies of Italian Design in the Eighties.* Editor. Pansera, Anty. Milan: Alinari, 1983. pp. 21–36.

Filler, Martin. "Ambasz and the Poetics of Architectural Space." *Architecture and Urbanism* no. 155 (August 1983): pp. 62–66.

Filler, Martin. "Folk Art Museum's Striking New Tower." *House and Garden* (January 1983): p. 186.

Filler, Martin. "Journal: In Praise of Follies." *House and Garden* (December 1983): p. 216.

Fitch, James Marston. "Neither Reason nor Follies." *Metropolis.* November 1983, p. 15.

Il Disegno Industriale Italiano 1928–1981. Fratelli, Enzo. Torino, Italy: C.E.L.I.D., 1983. p. 117.

From the Spoon to the City. Curator. Venosta, Carla. Milan, Italy: Padiglione della Triennale, October 22, 1983.

Glancy, Jonathan. "Design Review: Milan Furniture Fair." *The Architectural Review* no. 1042 (December 1983): p. 74/12.

Halliday, Sarah. "Tour d'Objets: Ambasz at Krueger." *Skyline* (April 1983): p. 23.

Irace, Fulvio. "Follies." *Domus* no. 644 (November 1983): pp. 24–29.

Irace, Fulvio. "Paradise Lost... Garden Regained." *Emilio Ambasz: 10 Anni di Architettura, Grafica e Design.* Exhibition Poster. Milan: Centrodomus, 1983.

Irace, Fulvio. "L'Usine Verte." *Domus* no. 636 (February 1983): pp. 22–25.

It is Design. Curator. Pansera, Anty. Milan, Italy: Padiglione D'Arte Contemporanea, 1983.

Krug, Karl-Heinz. "Mehr Licht als Leuchte." *Form* (January 1983): pp. 10–13.

"Las 'Correspondencias' Entre Arquitectura y Escultura en la obra de Diez Grandes Artistas Contemporáneos." *Diario SUR* (February 3, 1983).

"Materialidea." *Space Design* no. 8303 (1983): pp. 13–20.

Melissa, Lilia. "Letter from New York: Italian 'New Design'." *Interni Annual '83* (1983): p. 23.

Mendini, Alessandro. "Colloquio con Emilio Ambasz." *Domus* no. 639 (May 1983): p. 1.

"Mostre: Emilio Ambasz." *Casa Vogue* no. 145 (October 1983): p. 190.

Nakamura, Toshio. "The Architecture of Emilio Ambasz." *Architecture and Urbanism* no. 155 (August 1983): pp. 36–61, 74–82.

"Orgatechnik—A Really Big Show." *Progressive Architecture* (January 1983): p. 27.

Portoghesi, Paolo. "Alle soglie del nuovo design." *Europeo* no. 43 (October 22, 1983): p. 109.

Schultz, Gisela. "Büroleuchten." *Moebel + Decoration* (April 1983): p. 75.

Sedofsky, Lauren. "New York New." *Paris Vogue* no. 640 (October 1983): p. 302.

Slavin, Maeve. "15 Honored at Big I Champagne Breakfast Gala." *Interiors* vol. 142. no. 9 (April 1983): pp. 110–113.

Slavin, Maeve. "Interiors Awards: Quartet of Designers Chooses the Big I's." *Interiors* (January 1983): pp. 94–118.

Slavin, Maeve. "People and Events: Honoring Ambasz." *Interiors* (November 1983): p. 20.

Txomin, Badiola. "5 Arquitectos, 5 Escultores en el Museo de Bellas Artes de Bilbao." *Fula del Oeio* (March 18, 1983).

Venosta, Carla. "From the Spoon to the Town: Through the Work of 100 Designers." *ICSID 1983 Congress.* Milan, Italy: Congress, 1983. pp. 26–27.

"Vertebra." *Design Furniture from Italy: Production, Technics and Modernity.* Stuttgart: Stuttgart Design Center (March/April 1983): pp. 92–93.

1982

"Architectura Latinoamericana Mostrada en Europa." *La Prensa.* Buenos Aires, Argentina: (July 6, 1982): p. 7.

"Arquitectura Latinoamericana Actual, esa Desconocida." *La Nación.* (July 9, 1982): p. 1.3a.

Bill, Max. "Design: In Weiss Farbiges Licht." *Form* no. 98 (February 1982): p. 48.

Bill, Max. "Personalien... aus der Design Szene: Emilio Ambasz." *Form* no. 98 (February 1982): p. 54.

Brosterman, Norman. "Folk Architecture." *Express* (Spring 1982): p. 21.

Buchanan, Peter. "Bank, Lausanne, Switzerland." *The Architectural Review* (August 1982): pp. 53–55.

Buchanan, Peter. "Contemporary de Chirico: Precursor to Post-Modernism." *The Architectural Review* no. 1025 (July 1982): pp. 46–47.

Busch, Akiko. "Contract and Residential Furniture." *Product Design* (1982–1983): pp. 105 and 141.

Busch, Akiko. "Home Electronics and Entertainment." *Product Design* (1982–1983): p. 85.

Collaborations: 5 Architects/5 Sculptors. Palacio de las Alhajas: Organizers and Producers. (Gimenez, Carmen, and Munoz, Juan.) Madrid, Spain, (November 1982).

Da Silva Ramos, Pamela. "Portraits D'Amerique." *Vogue Paris* no. 625 (April 1982): p. 218.

Dardi, Constantino. "Fink and Steiner House, Southampton, NY, Longarini House, Southampton, NY, Woods House New Canaan, Connecticut." *Domus* no. 628 (May 1982) pp. 16–21.

Daulte, Francois. "L'Art Vaudios dans une Banque Interna tionale." *L'Oeil* (March 1982): pp. 40–45.

Doubilet, Susan. "Cummins Appoints Ambasz." *Progressiv Architecture* (July 1982): p. 40.

Emery, Mare. "Banque Bruxelles Lambert, Lausanne Suisse." *L'Architecture d'Aujord'hui* no. 222 (Septembe 1982): pp. 88–89.

Fernandes, John C. "USA: La Valijita y el Courtain-Wall. *Vivienda* no. 235 (February 1982): p. 8.

Fernandez, Roberto. "Encuentros: Emilio Ambasz." *Do Puntos* no. 4 (March/April 1982): pp. 36–43.

Filler, Martin. "Gran Rifiuto on 53rd Street." *New York Art Journal* no. 14 (1982): pp. 32–34.

Filler, Martin. "Portraits D'Amerique." *Paris Vogue* (Apr 1982): pp. 214–228.

Giovanni, Odoni. "A Losanna, La Nuova sede di una Banca Prezisi Segreti." *Casa Vogue* no. 134 (October 1982 pp. 208–211.

Architecture in Latin America: Horizonte '82–IBA 84. C rator. Glusberg, Jorge. Berlin: Internationale Bauausste lung Berlin, 1982. p. 37.

Glusberg, Jorge. "Latinoamerica y su Arquitectura en Be lin." *Espacio* (September/October/November 1982 pp. 14–19.

Glusberg, Jorge. "Una Constante Búsqueda de la Poesia y l Auténticos Origenes de la Arquitectura." *Clarin Arqu tectura, Ingenieria, Planeamiento y Diseño* (February 1 1982): pp. 24–25.

Il Disegno del Prodotto Industriale: Italia 1860–1960. Gr gotti, Vittorio. Milano: Gruppo Editroiale Electa, 198 p. 392.

Guerra, Ramón. "5 Arquitectos, 5 Escultores." *062, Conse Superior de los Colegios de Arquitectos* (December 198 pp. 33–37.

Guisasa, Fèlix. "Correspondencias: 5 Arquitectos + 5 Esc tores." *Q* (December 1982): pp. 30–62.

Harvie, Ashley E. "Ambasz to Consult at Cummins Engin *Industrial Design Magazine* (July/August 1982): p. 13.

Klickowski, Hugo. "a/actualidad." *Ambiente* no. 33 (Aug 1982): pp. 7–8.

"Latinoamérica en Berlin." *Clarin* (June 11, 1982): p. 2.

Marin-Medina, Jose. "Una Propuesta de Cultura Arquit tónica." *Informaciones* (November 4, 1982): pp. 26–27

Materialidea Curators. Castelli, Livia, and Ruina, Er Milan, Italy: Padiglione D'Arte Contemporanea, Septe ber 1982.

Mazzocchi, Gianni. "Bank Landscape." *Domus* no. 629 (Ju 1982): pp. 56–57.

Morozzi, Cristina. "La Finta Pelle del Progetto." *Modo* no. (December 1982): pp. 60–62.

Pallasmaa, Juhani. "University of Houston College of Arc tecture Honors Studio." *Explorations—Löytöretk Houston Arkkitehtskoulun Opilastöitä* (1982): pp. 16–17.

Penney, Richard. "Diversity and Human Factors Emerg Furnishings Design." *Industrial Design Magazine* (S tember/October 1982): pp. 24–29.

Petrina, Alberto. "Reportaje: Emilio Ambasz." *Summa* 174 (May 1982): pp. 21–22.

Postmodern—L'Architettura Nella Societa Post-Industr Portoghesi, Paolo. Milan: Electra, 1982. pp. 106–107.

Pragnell, Peter. "Points of Interest: Up." *Skyline* (June 19 p. 8.

Rawson, Deborah. "Future Scenarios." *Gentlemen's Qu erly* (October 1982): pp. 240–243.

New American Art Museums. Searing, Helen. New Y Whitney Museum of American Art, 1982. p. 12.

Sisto, Maddalena. "Il Cubo Assente." *Casa Vogue* (M 1982): pp. 208–211.

Sisto, Maddalena. "Mostre: Sei Grandi Firme per Alcan dei Divanetti Rigidi ai Corridoi Molli." *Casa Vogue* 133 (September 1982): pp. 384–395.

Slavin, Maeve. "Cummins Taps Ambasz." *Interiors* 1982): p. 18.

Smith, Janet M. "Maker of Myths and Machines: An Interview with Emilio Ambasz." *Crit* no. 11 (Spring 1982): pp. 21–24.

Viladas, Pilar. "Mainly on the Plain—Banque Bruxelles Lambert, Lausanne, Switzerland." *Progressive Architecture* (April 1982): p. 72.

Wagner, Walter. "New York's Museum of Folk Art Introduces a Well Mannered Tower." *Architectural Record* (July 1982): p. 53.

Zevi, Bruno. "Dal Barocco alle Ande." *L'Expresso* (August 29, 1982): p. 75.

1981

Belloni, Arturo. "Prömiertes Design aus Italien Österreich Japan." *Moebel + Decoration* (December 1981): p. 65.

Blau, Douglas. "Emilio Ambasz." *Flash Art* no. 101 (January/February 1981): p. 51.

Brown, Terry. "An Architect's Dream: Ancient Simplicity Meets Modern Art." *Home Energy Digest* (Spring 1981): pp. 32–34.

Buchanan, Peter. "Reconnaissance: Houses for Sale." *The Architectural Review* no. 1007 (January 1981): pp. 5–8.

Carlsen, Peter. "Designing the Post-Industrial World." *Art News* (February 1981): pp. 80–86.

Casati, Cesare. "Columbus Il Mito." *La Mia Casa* no. 141 (October 1981): pp. 106–107.

Davidson, Spencer. "Cover Story: Land of Miracles." *Time* (August 17, 1981): p. 15.

Della Corte, Evelyn. "Product Review: Back to Economics." *Interiors* Vol. CXL. no. 12 (July 1981): pp. 60–61.

Diffrient, Niels et al. "Top Award: Logotec Spotlight Range." *Industrial Design Magazine, Designers Choice* (1981): p. 27.

lquezabal, Eduardo. "Compasso d'Oro 1981." *Summa* (December 1981): p. 19.

n Exhibition of Architectural Drawings and Models by Emilio Ambasz, Michael Graves, Leon Krier, Aldo Rossi. Boston, Massachusetts: Vesti Corporation, Fine Arts Management, 1981.

ller, Martin. "Harbinger: Ten Architects." *Art in America* (Summer 1981): pp. 114–123.

urniture by Architects: Contemporary Chairs, Tables, and Lamps. Cambridge, Massachusetts: Hayden Gallery, Massachusetts Institute of Technology, 1981.

lusberg, Jorge. "Emilio Ambasz en Buenos Aires." *Clarin Arquitectura, Ingenieria, Planeamiento y Diseño* (December 18, 1981): p. 1.

oldberger, Paul. "A Meeting of Artistic Minds." *The New York Times Magazine* (March 1, 1981): pp. 70–73.

rossman, Luis J. "Emilio Ambasz o la Inefable Presencia de la Arquitectura." *La Nación*. December 20, 1981, p. 1.3a.

ace, Fulvio. "Museum as Work of Art." *Domus* no. 615 (March 1981): pp. 13–16.

win, Susan Grant. "Art and Antiques: Drawing Towards a New Architecture." *Town and Country* Vol. 135. no. 5010 (February 1981): pp. 172–174.

aerker, Christa. "Wohnhäuser Wie Skulpturen-Wer Will Sie? Erdloch Vom Wunderkind." *Art* (February 1981): pp. 90–91.

orton, David A. "Innovative Furniture in America." *Progressive Architecture* Vol. LXII. no. 5 (May 1981): p. 36.

rtoghesi, Paolo. "L'Architettura: Ma la Casa è Finita Sototerra." *Europeo* no. 43 (October 26, 1981): p. 103.

erci, Anna. "Il Momento e le Opinioni: Diece Anni Dopo, il Design Italiano negli USA." *Architectural Digest* (September 1981): p. 40.

ssell, Beverly. "The Editor's Word: Winners." *Interiors* January 1981): p. 61.

aultz, Gisela. "Preiswert und Trotzdem Beweglich." *Moebel + Decoration* (February 1981): p. 36–37.

ith, Phillip. "Books." *Manhattan Catalogue* Vol. 3. No. 4 (April 1981): p. 41.

ith, Philip. "A Millenarian Hope: The Architecture of Emilio Ambasz." *ARTS* Vol. 55. no. 6 (February 1981): p. 110–113.

ith, Philip. "Viewpoints, Architects and Architecture: The Underground Activity of Emilio Ambasz." *Gentlemen's Quarterly* Vol. 51. no. 4 (April 1981): p. 30.

kin, Michael. "Il Principio Portico." *Gran Bazaar* (May/June 1981): pp. 112–114.

kin, Michael. "The Odd Couples." *The Village Voice* March 18–24, 1981, p. 78.

a-2: The International Exposition of International Architecture. Wroclaw, Poland: Museum of Architecture, une 6–September 6, 1981.

0

ses for Sale. Editor. Archer, B.J. New York: Rizzoli International Publications Inc., 1980, pp. 3–16.

her, B.J. "Houses for Sale." *Architecture and Urbanism* December 1980): pp. 81–112.

iti, Fiamma. "Che Bella Casa! L'Appendo al Chiodo." *Europeo* no. 44 (October 27, 1980): pp. 117–118.

e, Francois. "Aménagement de Banque, Milan." *L'Architecture d'Aujordhui* no. 210 (September 1980): pp. 70–73.

Blake, John E. "Look Who's Lighting Up Britain." *Design* no. 379 (July 1980): pp. 40–43.

Blumenthal, Max "Projet d'une Maison pour un Couple, a Cordobe, Espagne." *Techniques et Architecture* no. 331 (June/July 1980): pp. 118–119.

Crossley, Mimi. "Review: 'City Segments'." *The Houston Post*. November 30, 1980, p. 16AA.

Davis, Douglas. "Selling Houses as Art." *Newsweek* (October 27, 1980): p. 111.

Davis, Douglas. "The Solar Revolution." *Newsweek* (April 7, 1980): pp. 79–80.

Dean, Andrea O. "Luis Barragán, Austere Architect of Silent Spaces." *Smithsonian* vol. 11. no. 8 (November 1980): pp. 152–156, 158 and 160.

Dixon, John Morris. "Milan Bank: Correction." *Progressive Architecture* Vol. LXI. no. 4 (April 1980): p. 4.

Doubilet, Susan. "Castelli: It Ain't Necessary So." *Progressive Architecture* Vol. LXI, no. 12 (December 1980): p. 32.

"Emilio Ambasz: House for a Couple, Cordoba, Spain, Award." *Progressive Architecture* Vol. LXI, no. 1 (January 1980): pp. 94–95.

Esterow, Milton. "The Utopian and the Pragmatic." *Art News* Vol. 79. no. 9 (November 1980): pp. 14–15, 161.

Filler, Martin. "Eight Houses in Search of Their Owners." *House and Garden* Vol. 152. no. 12 (December 1980): pp. 104–105.

Foster, Douglas. "Images and Ideas: 'City Segments' Exhibition." *Architecture Minnesota* (August 1980): pp. 68–70.

Twentieth-Century Furniture. Garner, Philippe. New York: Van Nostrand Reinhold Company, 1980. p. 219.

Gehry, Frank et al. "The 27th P/A Awards, Architectural Design: Emilio Ambasz." *Progressive Architecture* (January 1980): pp. 94 95.

Horsley, Carter B. "N.Y. Show Turns Spotlight on Custom Single-Family Dwellings." *International Herald Tribune* (November 24, 1980): p. 165.

Horsley, Carter B. "Shop for a Custom House in an Art Gallery." *The New York Times*. (August 24, 1980), p. C–8.

Huxtable, Ada Louise. "Focus on the Museum Tower." *The New York Times*. (August 24, 1980): pp. C27–C28.

Irace, Fulvio. "Poetics of the Pragmatic: The Architecture of Emilio Ambasz." *Architectural Design* (December 1980): pp. 154–157.

Irace, Fulvio. "The Poetics of the Pragmatic." *Architecture and Urbanism* no. 116 (May 1980): pp. 55–60.

Johnson, Michael J. "Architecture for Sale at New York's Leo Castelli Gallery." *Architectural Record* (October 1980): p. 33.

Kosstrin, Jane et al. "Bad Press is Better than no Press at all, or so Speak the Wise Men of the Media." *Fetish* (Fall 1980): p. 4.

Larson, Kay. "Art: Architecture Invitational." *The Village Voice*. July 2–8, 1980, p. 48.

Maack, Klaus J. " 'High Tech'—eine Chance für das Design?" *Form* no. 89 (January 1980): pp. 7–8.

Maack, Klaus-Jürgen. "Logotec-Design: Emilio Ambasz and Giancarlo Piretti." *ERCO Lichtbericht* (April 1980): pp. 12–13.

Mendini, Alessandro. "Elliptical Section Spot." *Domus* no. 605 (April 1980): p. 40.

Mendini, Alessandro. "Houses for Sale." *Domus* no. 611 (November 1980): pp. 30–32.

Mendini, Alessandro. "Museo in Torre." *Domus* no. 612 (December 1980): p. 33.

Miller, Nory. "Black Ribbons and Lace." *Progressive Architecture* Vol. LXI. no. 3 (March 1980): pp. 98–101.

Minardi, Bruno. "The Myth of the Cave." *Domus* no. 608 (August 1980): pp. 20–23.

Mosquera, Lala Méndez. "Diseño de Interiores, Línea Vértebra." *Summa* no. 157 (December 1980): pp. 93–95.

Nakamura, Toshio. "Special Issue: Emilio Ambasz." *Architecture and Urbanism* (May 1980): pp. 33–60.

Papademetriou, Peter C. "Inside 'Inside Outside'." *Texas Architect* Vol. 30. no. 4 (July/August 1980): pp. 79–81.

Pasta, Adriano. "Ristrutturazione della Banca Bruxelles Lambert a Milano/Interior Alterations for a Bank in Milan." *L'Industria delle Construzione* no. 108 (October 1980): pp. 5–8.

Pietrantoni, Marcello. "Fairy-Tale and Ritual." *Domus* no. 603 (February 1980): pp. 33–36.

Post, Henry. "Good Housekeeping, or Gimme Shelter." *New York* Vol. 14. no. 1 (December 29, 1980): p. 28.

Rense, Paige. "Emilio Ambasz: House for a Couple in Cordoba, Spain." *Architectural Design* (December 1980): pp. 152–153.

Schultz, Gisela. "Ein Stuhl der 'Lebt'." *Moebel + Decoration* (August 1980): pp. 44–45.

Smith, C. Ray. "Underground Buildings." *House and Garden, Building and Remodeling Guide* Vol. 1. no. 6 (November/December 1980): pp. 106–107.

Sorkin, Michael. "The Architecture of Emilio Ambasz." *Architecture and Urbanism* no. 116 (May 1980): pp. 36–39.

Sorkin, Michael. "Drawings for Sale." *The Village Voice*. November 12–18, 1980, pp. 85–86.

Sutphen, Melissa. "High Finance in a Stage Set." *Interiors* (June 1980): pp. 62–65.

Wiseman, Carter. "Having Fun with Classics." *New York* Vol. 13. no. 39 (October 6, 1980): pp. 35–43.

1979

Blumenthal, Max. "Deux Propositions Alternatives." *Techniques et Architecture* no. 325 (June/July 1979): pp. 101–104.

Carlsen, Peter, and Friedman, Dan. "The First 50 Years." *Gentlemen's Quarterly* Vol. 49. no. 9 (November 1979): pp. 146–151.

Casati, Cesare. "Concorso pro Memoria in Germania." *Domus* no. 598 (September 1979): pp. 40–41.

Casati, Cesare. "Per una Piccola Cooperativa." *Domus* no. 594 (May 1979): pp. 38–40.

Constantine, Eleni. "Artistic Alternates to Modernism Architectural Projects by Roger Ferri and Allan Greenberg Museum of Modern Art, New York June 2–July 25." Progressive Architecture Vol. LX. no. 7 (July 1979): p. 30.

Dixon, John Morris. "Working the Land." *Progressive Architecture* Vol. LX. no. 7 (April 1979): pp. 142–143.

Filler, Martin. "Interior Design: On the Threshold." *Progressive Architecture* Vol. LX. no. 9 (September 1979): p. 129.

Filler, Martin. "Rooms Without People: Notes on the Development of the Model Room." *Design Quarterly* no. 109 (1979): pp. 4–15.

Gregotti, Vittori. "Le Grandi Matito Sono Spuntate." *dell'Esspresso* (March 4, 1979): pp. 176–177.

Irace, Fulvio "C'era una Volta un Luogo un Cliente e un Architetto." *Modo* no. 22 (September 1979): pp. 31–36.

Metamorphosis 1978, McDonalds' Competition. Editor. Laine, Christian K. The Association of Student Chapters, American Institute of Architects, 1979.

Permar, Mary Elizabeth. "The Most Innovative McDonalds of the Future." *Crit* no. 5 (Spring 1979): pp. 26–27.

Stephens, Suzanne. "Book of Lists." *Progressive Architecture* Vol. LX. no. 12 (December 1979): pp. 56, 59.

1978

Ashton, Dore. "The Art of Architectural Drawings: A Review of a Show of Architectural Drawings and Models." *Artscanada* Vol. 35. no. 218/219 (February/March 1978): pp. 34–37.

Casati, Cesare. "Architettura: Come Disegnano Gli Architetti." *Domus* no. 578 (January 1978): p. 4.

Davis, Douglas. "Paper Buildings." *Newsweek* (February 6, 1978): pp. 76–77.

"Design Directions: Other Voices." *The AIA Journal* Vol. 67. no. 6 (Mid-May 1978): p. 160.

Fitzgibbons, Ruth Miller. "Body Furniture in the News." *House and Garden* Vol. 150. no. 8 (August 1978): pp. 108–109.

Gropp, Louis Oliver. "Color Abets Form for Mexican Architect." *A House and Garden Guide to Decorating* (Summer 1978): pp. 68–69.

Kubát, Bohumil. "Suet Nábytku." *Umenní a Remesla* (March 1978): pp. 56–58.

Contemporary Authors. Editor. Locker, Frances Carol. Detroit: Gale Research Company, 1978. Vols. 73–76: pp. 19–20.

Morton, David. "Emilio Ambasz: Poetic Pragmatics." *Progressive Architecture* (September 1978): pp. 98–101.

Raggi, Franco. "Emilio Ambasz: Una Relazione Sul Mio Lavoro." *Architecture Urbane Alternative Suburbane.* Venezia: La Biennale di Venezia, 1978. pp. 106–111.

Rose, Barbara. "The Fine Italian Hand." *Vogue* Vol. 168. no. 4 (April 1978): pp. 247–248, 320 and 322–323.

Scäfer, Sabine. "Forum Unberührt." *Bauen + Wohen* (January 1978): p. 3.

Vergottini, Bruno, and Iliprandi, Giancarlo. *New York, Inclusive Tour.* Naples, Italy: Alberto Marotta Editore S.P.A., 1978.

1977

Alexandroff, Georges. "Centre d'Informatique, Park 'Las Promesas,' Mexico City." *L'Architecture d'Aujourd'hui* Vol. 192. (September 1977): pp. 18–21.

Bauman, Horst H. et al. "Bürostühle aus einer Initiative." *Form* no. 79 (March 1977): pp. 34–35.

Sistemos de Significacion en Arquitectura. Bonta, Juan Pablo. Barcelona: Gustavo Gili, 1977. pp. 69, 257.

Casati, Cesare. "Underground Farm." *Domus* no. 576 (November 1977): pp. 41–43.

Dixon, John Morris. "Elusive Outcome." *Progressive Architecture* Vol. LVIII. no. 8 (May 1977): p. 90.

"Emilio Ambasz." *Architecture Organizer*: Apraxine, Pierre. New York: Leo Castelli Gallery, 1977. pp. 6, 7.

"Emilio Ambasz: Le Designer comme Réalisateur." *L'Architecture d'Aujourd'hui* no. 193 (October 1977): pp. 64–66.

Print Casebooks 2 The Best in Exhibition Design. Fox, Martin. Second Annual Edition. Washington, D.C.: RC Publications, Inc., 1977. p. 14–16.

Goldberger, Paul. "Architectural Drawings Raised to an Art." *The New York Times*. (December 12, 1977).

Hess, Thomas B. "Drawn and Quartered." *New York* Vol. 10. no. 41 (October 10, 1977): pp. 70–72.

Huxtable, Ada Louise. "Architectural Drawings as Art Gallery Art." *The New York Times*. (October 23, 1977), p. D-27.

Nakamura, Toshio. "Emilio Ambasz." *Shinkenchiku* (December 1977): pp. 186–187.

Design Review: Industrial Design 23rd Annual. Editor. Nydele, Ann. New York: Whitney Library of Design, 1977. p. 160.

Ponti, Gio. " 'Vertebra' Seating System." *Domus* no. 572 (July 1977): pp. 38–39.

Reif, Rita. "Swivel, Whirl, Rock and Roll—In Comfort." *The New York Times*. (June 30, 1977): p. 6.

Russell, Beverly. "How to Beat Backaches and Pains in a New Hot Seat." *House and Garden* Vol. 149. no. 3 (March 1977): p. 130.

Stern, Robert A.M. "Architects of the New '40 under 40'." *Architecture and Urbanism* no. 77 (January 1977): pp. 72–73.

"Vertebralement Bien Assis." *Vogue Hommes* (September 20, 1977).

Waisman, Marina. "La Arquitectura Alternativa de Emilio Ambasz." *Summarios* no. 11 (September 1977): pp. 29–32.

1976

Bendixson, Terrence. "Taxi: The Taxi Project: Realistic Solutions for Today." *RIBA Journal* (December 1976).

Casati, Cesare. "In Peru: Floating Units." *Domus* no. 555 (February 1976): pp. 30–31.

"Community Arts Center." *Space Design* no. 146 (October 1976): pp. 13–19.

"A Cooperative of Mexican-American Grape Growers." *Space Design* no. 146 (October 1976): pp. 8–12.

"Crate Containers, Italy: The New Domestic Landscape." *Space Design* no. 146 (October 1976): pp. 28–29.

Donovan, Hedley. "Call Me a Taxi, You Yellow Cab." *Time* Vol. 107. no. 26 (June 21, 1976): pp. 60–61.

"Ecco il Taxi Alfa Romeo." *Corriere della Sera* (June 6, 1976).

"Educational and Agrarian Community Centers." *Space Design* no. 146 (October 1976): pp. 20–27.

"Emilio Ambasz A Beaux-Arts Courthouse in Grand Rapids, Mich." *Progressive Architecture* Vol. LVII. no. 1 (January 1976): pp. 60–61.

"Emilio Ambasz Village des Chicanos." *L'Architecture d'Au-*

jourd'hui no. 186 (August/September 1976): pp. 70–72.

Europa-America: Architetture Urbane/Alternative Suburbane. Venice: The Venice Biennale, Magazzini del Sale alle Zattere, 1976.

"Giugiaro: proposta di un Taxi per gli tanni o Hanta!" *Il Fiorino* (June 20, 1976).

Hasegawa, Aiko. "Special Feature: Up-and-Coming Light: Emilio Ambasz—His Works and Thoughts." *Space Design* no. 7610 (October 1976): pp. 4–44.

Kicked a Building Lately? Huxtable, Ada Louise. New York: Quadrangle/The New York Times Book Company, 1976. pp. 51, 205 and 207.

"Invisible Storage." *House and Garden* Vol. 148. no. 8 (August 1976): pp. 64–67.

Kron, Joan. "The Tip off on Taxi Interactions." *New York* Vol. 9. no. 25 (June 21, 1976): p. 50.

Moore, Arthur Cotton et al. "23rd Annual Awards—Emilio Ambasz." *Progressive Architecture* (January 1976): pp. 60–61.

Mosquera, Lala Méndez. "Distinciones a Arquitectos Argentinos: Emilio Ambasz." *Summa* no. 103 (August 1976): p. 14.

Négréanu, Gérard. "Projet d'Équipements de Secours pour Zones Inondées." *CREE* (December 1975/January 1976): pp. 61–63.

"Oporta Giugiaro." *Autosprint* (July 6, 1976).

Ponti, Gio. "Taxi a New York." *Domus* no. 560 (July 1976): pp. 40–44.

Princeton's Beaux Arts and Its New Academicism from Labatut to the Program of Geddes. New York: The Institute for Architecture and Urban Studies, 1976.

Reiss, Bob. "I'll be Down to Get You in a Steam Taxi, Honey." *New York Magazine* vol. 19. no. 25 (June 21, 1976): pp. 44–47.

"Seating System 'Vertebra'." *Space Design* no. 146 (October 1976): pp. 30–33.

Tafuri, Manfredo. "Les Cendres de Jefferson." *L'Architecture d'Aujord'hui* Vol. 186. (September 1976): pp. 53–58.

Tafuri, Manfredo. "Emilio Ambasz: Villages des Chicanos." *L'Architecture d'Aujord'hui* Vol. 186. (September 1976): pp. 70–72.

Tallmer, Jerry. "Taxi, Mister?" *New York Post* (July 10, 1976): p. 32.

"The Taxi Project: Realistic Solutions for Today." *Space Design* no. 146 (October 1976): pp. 34–44.

"Un Taxi per gli USA Progettato a Torino." *La Stampa* (June 19, 1976).

"Uno Studii Internazionale: Taxi per New York." *Stampa Sera* (June 24, 1976): p. 3.

Zevi, Bruno. "Architettura: Piazza Italia è uno Stivale." *L'Espresso* (April 25, 1976): pp. 100–101.

1975

Casati, Cesare. "Edifici Mobili Galleggianti: A Centre for Applied Computer Research." *Domus* no. 546 (March 1975): pp. 1–4.

Casati, Cesare. "Recycling and Restoration." *Domus* no. 551 (October 1975): pp. 8–10.

The Print Casebooks The Best in Posters. Fox, Martin. First Annual. Washington D.C.: RC Publications, Inc., 1975 p. 6.

Hasegawa, Aiko. "Center for Applied Computer Research and Programming Park 'Las Promesas,' Outskirts of Mexico City, Mexico." *Space Design* no. 132 (August 1975) pp. 56–61.

Morton, David A. "Ultimately, a Flower Barge." *Progressive Architecture* Vol. LVI. no. 5 (May 1975): pp. 76–79.

Négréanu, Gérard. "Projet pour un Centre de Calcul á Mexico." *CREE* no. 36 (August/September 1975): pp. 66–67.

Négréanu, Gérard. "Projet d'Équipements de Secours pour Zones Inondées." *CREE* (December 1975/January 1976) pp. 61–63.

Ryder, Sharon Lee. "The Art of High Art." *Progressive Architecture* Vol. LVI. no. 3 (March 1975): pp. 62–67.

1974

Design. Noblet, Jocelynde. Chéne, France: Editions Stock 1974. p. 371.

1971

Arquitectura: Forma de Conocimiento forma de Comunicacion. Portas, Nuno. Barcelona: Escuela Tecnica Superior de Arquitectura de Barcelona, February 1971. pp. 1 and 6.

1970

McQuade, Walter. "Pursuing the Poetic Artifact." *Porfoli* (October/November 1970): pp. 76–80.

1967

Kurtz, Stephen A. *Wasteland: Building the America Dream*. New York: Praeger Publishers, 1967.

PHOTO CREDITS

Project Credits

Lucile Halsell Conservatory
Client	San Antonio Botanical Center Society
Principal in Charge	Emilio Ambasz
Project Director	Dwight Ashdown
Glazing Consultant	Erik Hansell
Project Development	Alan Henschell
Design Team	Frank Venning
	Mark Yoes
Illustrator	Suns Hung

Center for Applied Computer Research
Client	Centro Mexicano de Calculo Aplicado S.A.
Partner in Charge	Emilio Ambasz
Design Team	Robert Hart
Illustrator	Lauretta Vinciarelli
Model Maker	L. Borda

Grand Rapids Art Museum
Client	Grand Rapids Art Museum
Partner in Charge	Emilio Ambasz
Line Drawings	Deborah Booher
Illustrators	Mark Mack
	Lauretta Vinciarelli

Cooperative of Mexican-American Grape Growers
Client	Cooperative of Mexican American Grape Growers
Partner in Charge	Emilio Ambasz
Line Drawings	Mark Mack
Illustrator	Noel Naprstilc

Banque Bruxelles Lambert, Milan
Client	Banque Bruxelles Lambert
Partner in Charge	Emilio Ambasz
Collaborator	G. Cicorella
Carpet	Louis De Poorter

Manoir d'Angoussart
Client	Baron & Baroness Philippe Lambert
Partner in Charge	Emilio Ambasz
Model Maker	Elio Bandini
Illustrator	Donald Cheriflein

Museum of American Folk Art
Client	The Museum of American Folk Art
Partner in Charge	Emilio Ambasz
Design Team	Michael Monsky
Illustrator	Suns Hung
Model Maker	N. Salvarani
Consultants	Michael Kwartler
	Thomas Jones

Casa de Retiro Espiritual
Client	(name witheld by request)
Partner in Charge	Emilio Ambasz
Line Drawings	Robert Hart
Illustrator	L. Mattei
Model Maker	N. Salvarani

Co-Memoria Gardens
Client	Ludenhausen Township, West Germany
Partner in Charge	Emilio Ambasz
Illustrator	L. Mattei

Banque Bruxelles Lambert, Lausanne
Client	Banque Bruxelles Lambert
Partner in Charge	Emilio Ambasz
Collaborator	Andrea Penzo

Houston Center Plaza
Client	Texas Eastern Corporation
Partner in Charge	Emilio Ambasz
Project Director	Dwight Ashdown
Design Team	Richard Rudman
	Ann Cederna
	Toshio Okumura
	Jonathan Marvel
Model Maker	Daniel Trupiano

Schlumberger Research Laboratories
Client	Schlumberger Corporation
Partner in Charge	Emilio Ambasz
Project Architect	Dwight Ashdown
Design Team	Richard Rudman
	Ann Cederna
Model Maker	Daniel Trupiano

House for Leo Castelli
Client	Leo Castelli
Partner in Charge	Emilio Ambasz
Illustrator	Arthur Arnold
Model Maker	Daniel Trupiano

Plaza Mayor
Client	City of Salamanca
Partner in Charge	Emilio Ambasz
Project Director	Dwight Ashdown
Assistant	Faye Schultz
Illustrator	Suns Hung

Banque Bruxelles Lambert, New York
Client	Banque Bruxelles Lambert
Partner in Charge	Emilio Ambasz
Project Director	Robert Krone
Project Team	Ann Cederna

Elective Affinities
Client	Milan Triennale, 1985
Partner in Charge	Emilio Ambasz
Project Director	Joan Blumenfeld
Illustrator	Suns Hung

New Orleans Museum of Art
Client	New Orleans Museum of Art
Partner in Charge	Emilio Ambasz
Project Director	Dwight Ashdown
Design Team	Richard Rudman
	Ann Cederna
Illustrator	Dwight Ashdown
Model Maker	Dwight Ashdown

Emilio's Folly: Man is an Island
Client	Castelli Gallery
Partner in Charge	Emilio Ambasz
Illustrator	Dwight Ashdown
Model Maker	Toshio Okumura

Eschenheimer Tor
Client	City of Frankfurt
Partner in Charge	Emilio Ambasz
Project Director	Dwight Ashdown
Design Team	Lidia Heres
	Thomas Rainer Fischer
Illustrator	Suns Hung

Financial Guaranty Insurance Company
Client	Mr. Gerald Friedman President of FGIC
Principal	Emilio Ambasz
Project Director Phase I	Joan Blumenfeld
Project Director Phase II	Evan Douglis
Project Team	Gary Chan
	Mark Robbins
	Ken Laser
	Terry Kleinberg
	Dominique Nerfin
Assistants	Brian McGrath
	Margaret Mamboubin
	Wilcox Dunn
	Ben Puranan
	Mercedes Del Rio
	Veronique Demarel

Mercedes Benz Showroom
Partner in Charge	Emilio Ambasz
Project Coordinator	Evan Douglis
Assistant	Gary Chan
Professional Consultant	Erik Hansell
Model Maker	George Rastialla

Residence au-Lac
Client	Gianluigi Caverzasio
Partner in Charge	Emilio Ambasz
Design Team	Ann Cederna

Master Plan for the Universal Exhibition—Seville 1992
Client	City of Seville
Partner in Charge	Emilio Ambasz
Project Director	Dwight Ashdown
Design Team	Guillermo de la Calzada
	Katherine Keane
	Jonathan Marvel
	Dominique Nerfin
	Peter Robson
Assistants	Gary Chan
	Evan Douglis
Illustrator	Suns Hung
Model Makers	Daniel Gallagher
	Andreas Gruber

Frankfurt Zoo
Client	City of Frankfurt
Partner in Charge	Emilio Ambasz
Project Director	Dwight Ashdown
Design Team	Richard Barrett
	Thomas Fischer
Illustrator	Suns Hung
Model Maker	Andreas Gruber

Nichii Obihiro Department Store
Client	Nichii Company
Partner in Charge	Emilio Ambasz
Project Director	Dwight Ashdown
Design Team	Chung Nguyen
	Ira Frazin
	Katherine Liu
Illustrator	Suns Hung
Model Maker	Umit Koroglu
	Brad Whitermore
	Stanley Stinnett

Union Station
Client	Kansas City Corporation for Industrial Development
Partner in Charge	Emilio Ambasz
Project Director	Dwight Ashdown
Design Team	Chung Nguyen
	Ira Frazin
	Katherine Liu
Illustrator	Suns Hung
Model Maker	Zelvin Models

Vertebra
Co-designer	Giancarlo Piretti
Manufacturer	Argentina/Erasmo
	Italy/Castelli
	Japan/Itoki
	United States/Krueger

Dorsal
Co-designer	Giancarlo Piretti
Manufacturer	Canada/Global
	England/Antocky Lairn
	France/Eurosit
	Germany/Vitra
	Italy/COM
	Japan/Itoki
	United States/Krueger

Lumb-R Seating
Manufacturer	Vitra

L-System
Manufacturer	Herman Miller, Inc.

N14 Liter Automotive/Industrial Diesel Engine
Chief Engineer	John Stang
Associate Engineer	J. Hamilton

Escargot Air Filter
Manufacturer	Fleetguard

Logotec Spotlight
Co-designer	Giancarlo Piretti
Manufacturer	ERCO Leuchten GmbH

Oseris
Co-designer	Giancarlo Piretti
Manufacturer	ERCO Leuchten GmbH

Agamennone
Manufacturer	Artemide

Soffio
Manufacturer	Sirrah

Flexiboll
Manufacturer	Pentel

Toothbrushes
Manufacturer	Sunstar

Vittel Water Bottle
Manufacturer	Vittel

Aquacolor
Manufacturer	Herlite GmBH

Polyphemus
Manufacturer	G.B. Plast

PROJECT INDEX

ARCHITECTURE

EXHIBIT DESIGN

INDUSTRIAL DESIGN

GRAPHIC DESIGN